A Road Map to PLC Success

Educators often have trouble properly implementing Professional Learning Communities (PLCs) because they simply don't know *how* the process is supposed to work. By cutting through the fluff and generalities, this book provides a clear road map that takes school leaders step-by-step through the entire PLC process. Each chapter addresses a foundational component or protocol necessary for building successful team-based learning communities, using real-life examples to help teachers and leaders understand how to integrate this process and avoid common pitfalls that inhibit implementation. Whether you're just starting the PLC process or you're looking to get more out of your PLCs, this book will lead you to continued student and teacher growth, regardless of current achievement levels, socioeconomic status, or impending curricular changes.

Dr. Sean McWherter is Executive Director of Support Services for Asheboro City Schools, North Carolina, USA.

Other Eye On Education Books
Available from Routledge
(www.routledge.com/eyeoneducation)

Ten Steps for Genuine Leadership in Schools
David M. Fultz

College for Every Student: A Practitioner's Guide to Building College and Career Readiness
Rick Dalton and Edward P. St. John

Leading Learning for ELL Students: Strategies for Success
Catherine Beck and Heidi Pace

Leadership in America's Best Urban Schools
Joseph F. Johnson, Jr., Cynthia L. Uline, and Lynne G. Perez

The Power of Conversation: Transforming Principals into Great Leaders
Barbara Kohm

First Aid for Teacher Burnout: How You Can Find Peace and Success
Jenny G. Rankin

What Successful Principals Do! 199 Tips for Principals, 2nd Edition
Franzy Fleck

The Revitalized Tutoring Center: A Guide to Transforming School Culture
Jeremy Koselak and Brad Lyall

7 Ways to Transform the Lives of Wounded Students
Joe Hendershott

School Leadership through the Seasons: A Guide to Staying Focused and Getting Results All Year
Ann T. Mausbach and Kimberly Morrison

Distributed Leadership in Schools: A Practical Guide for Learning and Improvement
John A. DeFlaminis, Mustafa Abdul-Jabbar, and Eric Yoak

The Leader's Guide to Working with Underperforming Teachers: Overcoming Marginal Teaching and Getting Results
Sally Zepeda

Five Critical Leadership Practices: The Secret to High-Performing Schools
Ruth C. Ash and Pat H. Hodge

Strategies for Developing and Supporting School Leaders: Stepping Stones to Great Leadership
Karen L. Sanzo

A Road Map to PLC Success

Sean McWherter

NEW YORK AND LONDON

First published 2017
by Routledge
711 Third Avenue, New York, NY 10017

and by Routledge
2 Park Square, Milton Park, Abingdon, Oxon, OX14 4RN

Routledge is an imprint of the Taylor & Francis Group, an informa business

© 2017 Taylor & Francis

The right of Sean McWherter to be identified as the author of this work
has been asserted by him in accordance with sections 77 and 78 of the
Copyright, Designs and Patents Act 1988.

All rights reserved. No part of this book may be reprinted or reproduced or
utilised in any form or by any electronic, mechanical, or other means, now
known or hereafter invented, including photocopying and recorcing, or in
any information storage or retrieval system, without permission in writing
from the publishers.

Trademark notice: Product or corporate names may be trademarks or
registered trademarks, and are used only for identification and explanation
without intent to infringe.

Library of Congress Cataloging in Publication Data
A catalog record for this book has been requested

ISBN: 978-1-138-22354-7 (hbk)
ISBN: 978-1-138-22355-4 (pbk)
ISBN: 978-1-315-40442-4 (ebk)

Typeset in Optima
by Deanta Global Publishing Services, Chennai, India

Visit the eResources: www.routledge.com/products/9781138223554

Contents

Preface	vii
Acknowledgments	xii
Meet the Author	xiii
eResources	xiv

1. What Page Are You On? — 1

Expectations   1
Common Terms with Uncommon Meanings   3
Conclusion   6

2. Getting Started — 8

Logistics   9
Conclusion   14

3. Understanding the Process—Part 1 — 15

Pace Yourself   15
Conclusion   32

4. Understanding the Process—Part 2 — 34

Common Assessments   34
Conclusion   47

5. Understanding the Process—Part 3 — 49

Using the Data   49
Conclusion   72

6. Guiding the Conversation — 74

Introduction   74
The First Meeting   74
Conclusion   83

Contents

7. Avoiding Common Pitfalls 84

Introduction 84
Focus on Core Instruction 84
Collaboration 87
Conclusion 97

8. Putting It All Together 98

Mapping out the Process, Foundations, and Protocols 98

Appendix 105

Preface

What makes Professional Learning Communities so great? Sure, all educators know of them, talk about them, and supposedly do them—but why? What is it about this process that compels school districts across the nation to operate as Professional Learning Communities (PLCs)? I'll cut right to the point, if done correctly the PLC process is the single most powerful system of protocols that guarantees continued teacher and student growth while also providing the required foundation to successfully assess and implement future curricular and student-centered learning initiatives.

So where is all the growth, why are schools and districts still struggling with implementing PLCs, and why is a process that holds such growth potential for both students and educators surrounded by so much ambiguity? Part of the reason for this is that we have come to a point where the term "PLC" is used to describe every conceivable type of casual conversation and regular team meeting(s). Teams meet in PLCs, but nothing has changed from when these same meetings went by a different name.

There is also the misconception that any type of collaboration constitutes a PLC, regardless of the topic—field trips, duty rosters, general curricular changes, who's covered what chapters, classroom management. All valid reasons to collaborate, but none of these constitutes a PLC meeting. Meetings that hold the title of PLC should only be used to describe a data-driven meeting focused around a common assessment that is used to improve student learning through the utilization of clear, relevant, and timely data.

Often times schools and/or teams have trouble properly implementing PLCs because they simply don't know how the process is supposed to work. They may have been told what to do, but we're never shown or told them exactly how it's supposed to be done, or what steps have to be taken to put a proper foundation into place. Simply tell ng someone what the destination is doesn't necessarily direct him or her how to get there. I have spent the majority of my career raising student achievement by either implementing or correcting school-based PLCs by not just telling people *what* a PLC is supposed to do, but by focusing on *how* the process is done.

So, What Is This Book About?

I'm glad you asked...By cutting through the clutter and the obscurity, this resource will provide you with an articulated road map that will take you step-by-step through the entire PLC process and all of its protocols, while explaining each foundational component necessary to ensure that your PLC gets started on the right foot and continues to build the internal capacity necessary to ensure the continued development of this process and its protocols, so that you may understand how and why the process must become an integrated part of what educators do every day and not a separate entity or the all-dreaded "one more thing."

This resource will assist you in turning your PLCs into the well-oiled growth machines that they should be. I will advise you how to avoid common pitfalls and give you practical real-life examples to make this process as applicable and relevant as possible. Whether you are just beginning the process or looking to get more out of it, the information in these pages will put you on a guaranteed road to success. No matter what level you work at (elementary or secondary) or what your position (teacher, building-level administrator, or district-level supervisor), effectively and properly implementing the PLC process will promise continued student and teacher growth regardless of resources, current achievement levels, socioeconomic status, or impending curricular changes. This book will provide a resource that is easy to reference and can be used to logically and cohesively improve current practices.

Who Is This Book For?

This book is readily applicable to all educators (kindergarten through 12th grade) who are involved in, or want to be involved in, collaborative groups. Although all educators could utilize and benefit from this resource, the targeted audience is those who have the capacity or influence to bring

Preface

about change either at grade level, to a content area team, or at school(s) or district(s). Most commonly this would refer to teacher leaders, curriculum facilitators, assistant principals, principals, and/or district leaders, but it is not necessarily limited to these groups.

Organization and Chapter Overviews

This book has been organized to first provide the reader with the most foundational protocols and organizational structures in the PLC process. Each chapter then builds upon the foundational components with the goal of providing the reader with a logical step-by-step resource that is organized in a manner similar to how implementation would occur.

In order to assist the reader to quickly access and reference this book, resource chapter overviews have been provided. However, the necessity of understanding each component in the process should overshadow one's potential desire to skip to various sections without first reading the preceding chapters.

Chapter 1 What Page Are You On?

This is a brief chapter that reviews the expectations of a team, school, or district that wants to start or improve upon their PLC structure. This chapter also addresses common terms that will be used in the book.

Chapter 2 Getting Started

This chapter reviews the logistical considerations that have to be considered when implementing PLC. These are things that must be considered and addressed prior to starting the process.

Chapter 3 Understanding the Process—Part 1: Pace Yourself

This chapter reviews much of the foundational things—pacing guides, unpacking of standards, alignment of learning targets, curriculum guides,

Preface

and lesson plans—that a school needs to have in place in order for PLC meetings to occur in the manner they are supposed to. Many are often overlooked and cause numerous PLCs to fall short of their expectations.

Chapter 4 Understanding the Process—Part 2: Common Assessments

This chapter reviews the role and importance of common assessments in the PLC: everything from how they need to be planned, when they need to be created/ distributed, the general guidelines they should follow (such as length and standards), and how they can be interna lly vetted. This chapter also considers and explains the setting of proficiency rates and establishment of reassessment protocols.

Chapter 5 Understanding the Process—Part 3: Using the Data

This chapter progresses and builds upon the previous one by explaining how the data from the common assessments can be easily and efficiently used to swiftly support students and improve student learning. This chapter also discusses the use of an intervention block to support the PLC process and gives examples of how schools can make the most use of their existing resources.

Chapter 6 Guiding the Conversation

This chapter walks through multiple PLC meetings to give a clear picture of what they are supposed to look like and what they can realistically accomplish, starting with the first meeting of the year and progressing through the third (after which the framework falls into a repeating cycle).

Chapter 7 Avoiding Common Pitfalls

This chapter gives advice for avoiding common mistakes that can hamper or derail the process. It also gives alternative avenues of implementation if a team, school, or district doesn't have the proper foundations in place to fully integrate the PLC process.

Chapter 8 Putting It All Together

This, the final chapter, pulls everything together and provides a concise overview of the process.

Special Features

This book contains many resources that will be useful to the reader. The content covers a well-known topic differently than it has ever been covered before. This difference is highlighted in specific examples and descriptions that allow school leaders to understand the logistical foundation that must be in place for their PLCs to be successful.

All of the content in this book is simply stated and has clear descriptions and templates that give precise examples to readers while also providing them with a usable resource. This book provides a number of templates, diagrams, and resources in order to afford the reader a logical step-by-step understanding of the entire PLC process and its components.

The examples utilized in this book can be easily adapted or modified to fit into any school setting regardless of resources. It was my goal throughout this entire book to continually move beyond simply telling the reader *what* a PLC is supposed to do, and inform them *how* they can actually accomplish it.

Acknowledgments

First and foremost I would like to acknowledge and thank you, the reader, for time and dedication to your students, colleagues, and staff members, and for recognizing that our craft is made better through collaboration.

I would also like to acknowledge my wife, Angie, for her endless love and support, for which I am truly blessed.

I would also like to say thank you to those principals and educators who had a direct hand in either assisting with proofreading various chapters, providing feedback, or allowing me to showcase their work within these pages. Thank you Katheryn Green, Julie Bachman, Christa DiBonaventura, Wende Henderson, Valerie Feezor, April Willard, Gordon Palmer, Leah Leonard, Tina Lupton, Heather McDonald, Heidi Pegram, and Neelam Awan. I would also like to say very special thank you to Christie Weatherly whose encouraging comments and desire are what initially lead me down the path to write this book (you are truly the embodiment of a great educator).

Also, a special thank you to Heather Jarrow and the folks at Routledge for supporting this work.

Meet the Author

Dr. Sean McWherter has had the opportunity to directly serve disadvantaged students in kindergarten through 12th grade settings. He received his doctorate in Educational Leadership from Gardner-Webb University in 2012 and was a school-based administrator in both a high school and an elementary school prior to becoming a district-level administrator. He has successfully utilized, and trained others on the implementation of, Professional Learning Communities as a mechanism for student growth, and believes that data-driven collaboration is the cornerstone to success.

Dr. McWherter lives in North Carolina with his loving wife and son.

eResources

Keep an eye out for the eResources icon throughout this book, which indicates a resource is available online. Resources mentioned in this book can be downloaded, printed, used to copy and paste text, and manipulated to suit your individualized use. You can access these downloads by visiting the book product page on our website:

www.routledge.com/products/9781138223554.

Then click on the tab that reads "eResources" and select the file(s) you need. The file(s) will download directly to your computer.

Tool		Page
• Figure 3.4	Curriculum Guide Template (A)	28
• Figure 3.5	Curriculum Guide Template (B)	29
• Figure 5.7	RIME Time	58
• Figure A1	Sample Data Form 1	105
• Figure A2	Sample Data Form 2	106
• Figure A3	Sample Elementary Master Schedule – Submitted by Denton Elementary, Davidson County	107
• Figure A4	Sample Elementary Master Schedule – Submitted by Midway Elementary, Davidson County	109
• Figure A6	8th Grade targeted instruction groups	112
• Figure A7	Sample Middle School Master Schedule – Submitted by E. Lawson Brown Middle School, Davidson County	114
• Figure A8	Targeted Instruction Lesson Outline	115

# What Page Are You On?

Expectations

Before we get too far into transforming your school with the power of PLCs, we need to ensure that we are on the same page concerning expectations and terms. First and foremost, we need to establish an expectation. This expectation is that you are going to be an active participant in this process, no matter what your role is. Sit and get doesn't get it; if you want results from this process you have to be active and involved in this process. Second, there are no half measures and this is not "one more thing." In a recent training, when asked to reflect on what they knew about PLCs one of the principles stated that "PLCs are a way of life, you don't just do it, you live it." If you are not whole-heartedly committed to student and teacher growth by identifying and integrating best practice through a collaborative and data-driven approach, then please stop reading now and put this book down.

> If you are still reading, then you are agreeing to be more than a spectator.

If you are still reading, then you are agreeing to be more than a spectator. You are agreeing to put into motion a process that has been identified as the surest, most promising, and universally accepted means of guaranteeing improved student and teacher performance and student growth (DuFour &

Eaker, 1998; Schmoker 2006). Make no mistake, it doesn't matter what our role is in education. We are all on the front line of doing the best we can for our students, and we all have a part to play. This book will make this process relevant to you no matter your position and no matter the resources or current achievement level of your school.

Once a school begins to properly implement PLCs the entire culture of the school will begin to shift. Your school will not just be data rich, as most already are, it will be data wise, knowing how to utilize and grow from the steady stream of high-quality data that this process will bring. Just as a race team responds to the data and places proper emphasis where it is needed each time a car hits the pit, a proper PLC knows how to appropriately calibrate itself each time a student or group of students has to make an academic pit stop.

If you are in a district-level leadership position, t is your responsibility to support this process and set a clear guideline of expectations to building-level administrators. These expectations must be measureable, and your school-based leaders must be held accountable. Don't be afraid to sit in on PLC meetings and give and receive feedback. Having the ability to freely circulate from school to school in these meetings will give you a clear picture of your district's strengths and weaknesses. You should then use this information to plan appropriate supports while also capitalizing on your district's internal strengths. You have to ensure that you have the ability, or can delegate the responsibility, to check on what you expect.

Also, as a district leader, it may be your responsibility to introduce this process to the principals or curriculum department. If you fail in delivering a logical and cohesive plan that people can commit to, then this process will be dead on arrival and will never take off in anything more than a name.

If you are a school-based administrator, it is your responsibility to lead your school in this cultural shift. You, or another school-based leader, must be present in the PLC meetings—being there once in a while or for a few minutes of an occasional meeting is a surefire way to sabotage this process. A school reflects its leader, and if you don't put an emphasis on this process with something more than words then don't expect your staff to.

Also, it is important for you to remember that you are there to "support" this process; you are not there to run it. If you are the main facilitator of every meeting, you are never going to give your staff the opportunity they need to stand on their own and be self-sufficient. A part of your leadership responsibility is to develop leadership in others. Over time your staff must be able to facilitate this process on their own. This process should not die simply because you are absent or relocate to a new position. There is also no reason a meeting should come to a halt simply because you have a last-minute emergency. Your goal is to assist each team in staying on target and keeping its conversation focused, while building its own capacity to function as a highly effective collaborative team.

If you are a teacher, it is your responsibility to be a team player. However, every team needs some type of leadership. Maybe you are, or are not, comfortable leading or facilitating these meetings; it matters not. What does matter is that you are an active and willing participant in this process. At times everyone in this process will have something to bring to the table; finding your voice at these times is critical. This can be daunting as many educators don't want to be viewed as cocky, arrogant, or a "know it all." A little bit of tact and respect can go a long way in this, but regardless, it is time to put the pettiness aside and remember that we are here to create the best learning environment possible for our students. This process is not about a specific individual on the team; it is about everyone coming together to do what is right.

Also, just like your supervisor, you are there to support this process. No one should have to tell you to put the laptop away, or to stop working on grades, or to come prepared. After your team sets up its norms, you must adhere to them. It is important that everyone leads by example in this manner. Remember, be the leader and coworker that you would like to have. Stay positive, be friendly and respectful, get to the point (tactfully), listen to what others have to share, and—most importantly—keep an open mind and be critical of what the data is telling you. There is going to be a wealth of knowledge in the room during every one of these meetings, and everyone is going to have something valuable to bring to the table.

Common Terms with Uncommon Meanings

Unfortunately, there tends to be a lot of of confusion and conflicting understandings regarding assessment types and their purposes. This, I believe, is largely due to differing internal beliefs that educators hold based on definitions that were previously used as functional terms (such as formal and informal assessments), coupled with slightly varying definitions and uses of terms between states, districts, schools, and even classrooms within the same building. I have seen and heard such a variety of interpretations of the terms formative assessment and summative assessment that it makes my head spin.

The reason I bring this issue to the forefront is that when educators have varying understandings of a term the meaning of an entire message or protocol can be misinterpreted. The reason this causes such an issue in the PLC process is that educators tend to apply their preferred definition to the literature despite the authors' best attempts to define how they are using the terms. Below I have briefly outlined some of the conflicting definitions regarding formative and summative assessments.

Formative Assessments

Educators across the spectrum present and cite varying definitions of formative assessments. Some identify them as being any assessment in which on-going data is used to inform instruction, or minute-to-minute assessments (North Carolina Department of Public Instruction). Others refer to them as assessments for learning. These definitions of the term are often hard for educators to grasp, as they represent a descriptive process that can encompass virtually every type of assessment format. Even DuFour et al. (2010), who supports the definitions presented above, acknowledges that there are varying operating definitions of formative assessments and that most research on formative assessment focuses on daily or ongoing assessments. These assessment types are often difficult to collect specific data on as they are not generally graded and can make a PLC look and sound different from an example one may read about.

According to this definitive process, I firmly believe that every assessment should be formative in nature. If we apply this definition according to its literal meaning, then a formative assessment should encapsulate virtually every type of assessment that a student takes as there should be no assessment that is given "just because" or whose data isn't used to improve instruction. The PLC process promotes data-driven decision-making using data from all assessment types. There is simply no reason that data from benchmarks and end-of-year assessments shouldn't be used to modify instruction while providing students with higher quality instruction just because they are not referred to as formative.

Summative Assessments

Many think that summative assessments are given at the end of an instructional standard or unit, or believe them to simply be the assessment they give when they are done teaching a particular topic, standard, or unit. Others operate under the assumption that the term only applies to assessments that educators don't do anything with—the "autopsy"—or that it is an assessment of learning, not for learning, and that teachers are mysteriously not permitted to use their data for learning...because then—oh wait—the assessment is back to being formative. This confliction actually begs a more serious question: why on earth would educators give an assessment that they are not going to use to educate...? Perhaps that's a discussion for another time. Others think that, regardless of what you do with them, summative assessments are only end-of-year assessments and/or benchmarks or midterm exams. I have even heard others say that summative only refers to those assessments that are district- or state-mandated.

One could easily chalk up these differences to mere semantics, and in many ways how these terms are utilized could be considered relatively inconsequential if, and only if, everyone in your district operates under the same norms and has a common understanding of the adopted terms, whatever they may be. I simply recommend that, regardless of which way your school, district, or state decides to define and operate these terms, do not simply assume that everyone has the same interpretation. You need to be aware of the way different and/or dated material refers to these terms, and be aware that this could cause some confusion to your teachers and staff. It may seem absurd that something as small as the simple use of terms could get in the way of a school's success, but without a common use and true understanding of applied terms the PLC process can easily become inert.

As a result of these pervasive differences, and to avoid any confusion or potential misinterpretations, I will use neither of these terms (formative or summative) from this point forward. When describing an assessment I will simply call it what it is, that is test, quiz, benchmark, or end-of-year assessment, and give an example of it to provide clarity. When talking about quizzes I may also refer to them as minor assessments and tests as major assessments—they are one and the same: quiz is a minor assessment, and test is a major assessment. This way, you may apply your own understandings and operating definitions without concern that we are or are not on the same page. In all actuality, it doesn't matter if you call your assessments apples and bananas so long as you apply them properly to the process.

Day-to-Day Assessment, Informal: A very brief assessment used by teachers and students during instruction in order to prov de instant feedback in order to immediately adjust teaching and learning.

Quizzes (Minor Assessment): An assessment administered within a unit of study to identify student learning at the end of an instructional skill or checkpoint. Many teachers give quizzes on a weekly basis. These are given after the completion of instruction and are used to monitor the effectiveness of one's instruction, as well as giving students a measurement of readiness for the next set of scaffold information.

Tests (Major Assessments): An assessment administered at the end of an instructional unit. A test generally includes information from multiple quizzes and serves as a checkpoint within an academic quarter or semester. These are also given after the completion of instruction and are used to monitor the effectiveness of one's instruction.

Benchmarks and End-of-Year Assessments: These are large assessments given to all students on a particular grade level or in a particular subject or class in order to monitor student readiness and, often, teacher effectiveness. These assessments are given only a few times a year, at pre-established times, and are commonly given at the district or state level.

Common Assessments: Any assessment can be a common assessment as long as it is the same assessment and is given after the same number of instructional days or during the same point of a lesson.

Conclusion

I hope this brief chapter has succeeded in putting us on the same page regarding the use of terms, while also providing a simple place to reference some of the key terms in this book that are usually associated with student learning and PLCs. You will also have recognized that this process involves everyone in the school and, like all books and professional development sessions and seminars, simply reading the book or attending the seminar will not make you or your school successful. Rather, the growth and success that you will experience is indicative of what you actually do with the new information you have attained.

References

DuFour, R., & Eaker, R. (1998). *Professional Learning Communities at Work: Best Practices for Enhancing Student Achievement.* Bloomington, IN: Solution Tree Press.

DuFour, R., DuFour, R., Eaker, R., & Many, T. (2010). *Learning by Doing: A Handbook for Professional Learning Communities at Work.* Bloomington, IN: Solution Tree Press.

North Carolina Department of Public Instruction. (n.d.). *Learn More About Formative Assessment.* Retrieved on 3 November, 2015 from http://www.ncpublicschools.org/accountability/educators/vision/formative on 3/5/15

Schmoker, M. (2006). *Results Now.* Alexandria, VA: ASCD.

2 | **Getting Started**

Before you can successfully begin the process for implementing PLCs, you must first understand their purpose and the necessary framework for completing that purpose. It is a shame that the term "Professional Learning Community" has come to describe every type of conceivable meeting including casual teacher conversations. In many cases, schools starting the PLC process simply substituted one name in for another with no actual change to their meetings. Like magic—poof!—what was a team meeting is now a PLC! Strange that a year later they're left scratching their heads, wondering why their students didn't show growth in learning.

Without a clear focus and a clear sense of direction, you cannot expect to increase student learning just because you start calling something by a different name. Simply calling a meeting a PLC does not make it so.

> Simply calling a meeting a PLC does not make it so.
>
> The sole purpose of a PLC is to utilize a data-focused approach to improve student learning.

The sole purpose of a PLC is to utilize a data-focused approach to improve student learning. It is not to discuss fieldtrips, the state playoffs, final-four tournaments, or recent weekend adventures and dramas. It is not a forum to complain about or blame students, parents, administrators, or the fact that you think you have more important things to do. You may think that you have better things to do than be in a PLC meeting, but the truth is—you don't. PLCs are quite simply the single most effective strategy for improving student and teacher growth. Remember, the focus is student learning, plain and simple. The "how" is what this book is all about.

Logistics

The logistical aspect of PLCs is imbedded in every part of the PLC process. However, a proper logistical framework will not necessarily guarantee your success. Whereas, the lack of a proper framework coupled with poor logistical foresight and an inability or unwillingness to adapt will guarantee failure, and may likely push you or your teachers to pursue an unhealthy drinking habit.

Before you start the PLC process, you must ensure that your school has established a logistical framework for success. This section will briefly review some of the basic components that should be identified and figured out prior to the first PLC meeting.

Planning Times: Teachers must have common planning times with their like-subject or grade-level peers. This may be difficult for some secondary schools in which teachers have multiple preps and may even teach multiple content areas. Organizing a school's master schedule to allow for common planning times has numerous benefits including instructional coordination and integration, as well as fostering peer learning and continuous improvement (Legters et al. n.d.; Desimone, 2002; Jackson & Bruegmann, 2009). No matter how much instructional support an administrator provides, teachers must have time to collaborate with each other. This is necessary in order to help teachers manage their own professional growth and build capacity (Jackson, 2012).

However, if the school is simply too large or if for some reason there is simply no plausible way you can coordinate common planning times with an entire grade level or content area, consider splitting them into logical teams, such as grouping those who teach a specific course or even those that may do cross-curricular theming. Common planning periods also provide a logical time to schedule your PLC meetings. Scheduling PLC meeting before or after school is another plausible idea, although one must be prepared to deal with complexities that will arise when team members either show up late or have to leave early.

Getting Started

Apart from being too big, another possible barrier to holding meaningful common planning times and PLC meetings is being too small. What do you do if you only have a couple of teachers per grade level, or they are departmentalized and there is only one teacher who teaches a subject? How can these meetings be organized so that the PLC process can still be beneficial? The scenarios below illustrate potential ways to overcome this challenge.

> **Scenario One:** Due to their small sizes, both Beaver Creek and Apple Valley elementary face this issue on a yearly basis as they have only one or two teachers per grade level. To further compound the problem of their small size, each school has recently decided to experiment with departmentalization. After analyzing multiple teacher and student data points, the schools decided to match their teachers with their strongest core competency. This decision was made in an effort to improve student learning.
>
> While the decision to do this was data based and in the best interests of the students, it did cause ogistical complications to the existing PLC process at each school. Although the schools still had common planning times, the teachers no longer had a peer in the building to collaborate with who was teaching the same grade-level content.
>
> In order to overcome this obstacle, the principals of each school decided to work together and coordinate the teacher planning periods and PLC meetings of their teachers with each other. Working together in this manner allowed opportunities for their teachers to videoconference with one another while also attending scheduled face-to-face meetings established by their principals. In order to maintain their PLC structure and develop their PLC fidelity, the principals were careful to align their PLC meeting structures with each other.
>
> These principals value collaboration and understand that in order to provide a relevant continuing growth environment for both their teachers and students an opportunity must exist for their teachers to collaborate and reflect with others teaching the same grade level and content area.

Getting Started

Scenario Two: Fledging Elementary provides another example of how to achieve meaningful common planning periods while overcoming low faculty numbers. Fledging Elementary currently has three teachers on most grade levels. However, because of departmentalization. The principal realized that the PLC team would be deprived of collaboration within core subject areas. After the adoption of a new curriculum it was evident that total integration would be required in all subjects to foster open dialogue during weekly PLC sessions. Teachers are expected, through the norming process they create at the beginning of the school year, to prepare rigorous lessons that reach various learners found within each specific group of students. Students move seamlessly between classes based on where they are in their learning process during each particular unit of study. Weekly discussions are driven by this organic placement of students in order to ensure students are in a learning group that best fits their academic needs.

Collaboration found within the PLC requires a true partnership between teachers to effectively teach core expectations. Integration is expected across all core subjects. Fledging Elementary has found that students are much more academically involved if what they learned in one teacher's class is also reviewed and explored with another classroom teacher. The partnership between teachers and the value of their lessons has become much richer, and teacher leadership capacity has shown tremendous growth. Student data is current and relevant and is used to drive each PLC meeting. This fluid and cross-curricular partnership has made this specific grade level a model in the district for grade-level collaboration.

Frequency of PLC Meetings: A schedule must be established that supports a minimum of one weekly PLC meeting for every PLC group. You may also need to establish two weekly meetings when first starting this process. Having a shared planning time among each PLC group will also allow teachers to work together on a daily basis and should increase their efficiency during the meeting.

Getting Started

When to Schedule the Meetings: As an administrator you really have only two viable options for scheduling PLC meetings.

Option 1: Pick a day out of the week that works for you and the majority of your teachers and set all meetings for a single day, if logistically feasible. If your school schedule will not accommodate a single-day model, try to reorganize to do so, or schedule the PLC meeting for a specific time each day so that there is never a question of when and where. This will also greatly help you with monitoring and providing support.

Option 2: Schedule the same block of time each day for each grade level or content area. For example, perhaps you can organize resources to provide each grade level an extra 40 minutes for planning first thing in the morning, and each grade level or content area has their PLC on a separate day. Another alternative is to provide each group with the opportunity to meet after school on a specific day.

Conversely, I've also found that when these meetings are held after school they are usually not as efficient and generally have lower staff participation. This can often be attributed to after-school activities such as clubs and athletics, and higher rates of teacher absences—needing to leave early to pick up their children, run errands, attend scheduled appointments, etc., etc. You may also run into conflicts with other professional developments and faculty meetings. For these reasons, I would generally advise against holding meetings after school.

However, this does not mean that you can't find success holding PLC meetings after school; just be aware of the possible road blocks and put measures in place to avoid unnecessary complications.

The day chosen to conduct PLC meetings will obviously vary from school to school, and a PLC held on a Wednesday isn't necessarily going to be more effective than one scheduled for a Thursday. Pick what works best for your school and staff, but make sure both you and your teachers can actually be in the meetings. So, if you feel confident in working these in after school, give it a shot. If you work with your teachers to pick the best time for your staff, you are likely to have more success than if you just make the decision without their input. Be strategic the first time around to mitigate potential problems. However, if the day or time that you establish ends up being problematic, it's not the end of the world, and you can always change it.

Just be sure that you avoid a situation where you let each team on your staff schedule their meeting time for whenever they want, as you'll never make it to all the meetings no matter how good your intentions are. In addition, if you provide each group with the opportunity to freely schedule, then you are also giving them the opportunity to freely reschedule. As such, you may find yourself arriving at a meeting only to find that it's been moved to a different day for x, y, or z reasons. If you let your staff autonomously schedule as they want, you will never be able to keep up.

Where to Hold the Meetings: In my experiences meetings are either held in a data room or a specific area or room in the school designated for PLCs or—if a space like this does not exist—then each team normally chooses one of their classrooms to hold the meeting. So long as everyone stays on task and the team is kept as free as possible from distractions, it doesn't really matter what venue you choose to use. In the end, logistics may prevent you from having a choice in the matter.

Just ensure that whatever room you choose meets the needs of the PLC. You should consider things such as wireless connection, projector, space, tables, and appropriate climate control—I know some schools, especially older ones, can have some very "special" heating, ventilation, and air conditioning (HVAC) issues.

Who's in the Meeting: It is mandatory that all teachers in a specific grade level (elementary) or that teach a specific course (secondary) are in attendance as these are the key players. An administrator or other school leader also needs to be in attendance in order to keep the team focused, answer questions, and assist in facilitating as necessary. Attending these meetings will offer an excellent perspective into the dynamics of each team and allow administrators and school leaders phenomenal learning opportunities. In fact, it is doubtful that you will ever have found yourself more in tune with the curricular and professional development needs of your teachers than you will after spending time in their PLCs.

It is recommended, but not always logistically possible, for specialized teachers such as those working with students with disabilities and reading specialists to attend the meeting as well. These professionals may be able to offer some unique insights and recommendations when discussing and modifying assessments, tasks, lesson plans, and remediation strategies, and possible intervention techniques.

Conclusion

The logistical components are some of the first mechanisms that need to be planned for, and any problems usually surface in an ongoing manner throughout the year. Hopefully, the different examples and scenarios provided conveyed that there isn't necessarily one right way or a single team composition that is best. Often times, we need to be creative and think outside the box when trying to create a fluid structure. You also have to recognize that it's okay to get it wrong. You may try a structure that looks great on paper, but just doesn't work in practice. If this happens, modify it so that it works for you and your school. Even if it does work, be sure to revisit it each year and look for ways to improve the logistical efficiency.

References

Desimone, L. (2002). How can comprehensive school reform models be successfully implemented? *Review of Educational Research, 72*(3), 433–479.

Jackson, K., & Bruegmann, E. (2009). Teaching students and teaching each other: The importance of peer learning for teachers. *American Economic Journal: Applied Economics, 1*(4), 85–108.

Jackson, R. (2012). *Never Underestimate Your Teachers: Instructional Leadership for Excellence In Every Classroom*. Alexandria, VA: ASCD.

Legters, N., Adams, D., & Williams, P. (DATE). Common planning: A linchpin practice in transforming secondary schools. Retrieved on 3 February, 2015 from https://www2.ed.gov/programs/slcp/finalcommon.pdf

3 | Understanding the Process—Part 1

Pace Yourself

There are many steps that comprise the PLC process and many norms that have to be in place in order to maximize efficiency and effectiveness. This chapter is going to focus on the framework of components necessary to successfully start and guide the PLC meeting process. Although many of these components overlap and some are difficult to do and discuss in complete isolation of each other, I will try to bring clarity to the importance and sequence of each of these components. Missing any one of these components could quite literally prevent all, or most, of the potential gains you may have hoped to achieve from utilizing PLCs.

It is not fair to our teachers or students that we begin a process that we ourselves don't clearly understand and have mapped out. You must take the time to understand the foundational supports necessary to sustain the PLC process in order to avoid unnecessary growing pains and inefficiencies within the process.

Pacing guides, curriculum guides, and learning targets play an important, but vastly underrated, role in the PLC process and can be quite beneficial in helping teams to stay focused.

Pacing Guide

Establish a pacing guide for the subject or content area to be discussed, for example Math, Language Arts, Science. It is likely that one already exists for your district; however, it is important for your team to review the pacing guide. A district-provided pacing guide should be exactly what the name

Understanding the Process—Part 1

implies: a "guide"; it should not be considered a law or an unbreakable decree. The reasons for this should be self-evident.

If the focus is on student learning, then modification to the guide should be an expectation and the guide should be considered a living document. We do not move through at a pre-established pace and ignore student learning simply for the justification of "covering the content." Teachers are not tasked with covering standards: they are tasked with teaching them. Sometimes teaching for student learning may take more or less time than what is allotted on the pacing guide.

It is better to teach four out of five standards well and actually have your students learn them than it is to cover all five and leave your students with a scattered and incomplete foundation. I cannot voice this more eloquently than Douglass Reeves (2010), "there is not a shred of evidence that covering the curriculum and checking off items on pacing charts is equivalent to student learning."

> "There is not a shred of evidence that covering the curriculum and checking off items on pacing charts is equivalent to student learning."
>
> —Douglass Reeves, 2010

Before a new quarter begins, your PLC should meet to discuss the pacing guide and tentatively plan the duration of time they need to teach each standard, goal, or skill. The team should have the flexibility to move these standards around in the time frame of that quarter (many traditional schools break each quarter up into nine-week intervals) or in the time span of each scheduled benchmark or midterm exam. This way, students will still have been taught each standard within the allotted period and their benchmark or midterm data will be reflective of actual teaching and learning. If teams begin incorporating standards from outside these time periods then the benchmarks and midterm assessments will not accurately measure how effective the instruction has been. The only exception to this would be if the benchmarks or midterms are cumulative in the sense that they measure all standards to be taught throughout the entire year; in these cases it would make no difference when each standard is taught so long as proper sequencing and scaffolding exists.

Another aspect to creating and/or analyzing pacing guides that one must remember is that pacing guides are organized by standards, not by stories and books. We do not teach stories; we use stories to teach standards, concepts, and skills. For some teachers, especially those in Language Arts, this may be a departure from how they learned to teach and were themselves taught as children.

Traditionally, a story or book is taught and the standards for that quarter or the whole year are haphazardly covered wherever a teacher can fit them in. Or a story is taught from the schools Language Arts' textbook that has premade questions. It just so happens that those premade questions also cover an assortment of standards and are likely to be lacking in the required rigor. The book may also be dated and not even be properly aligned with current standards. This traditional method of teaching makes a data-focused approach to teaching and learning impossible to properly maintain because of its disjointed nature and scattered focus.

As the pacing guide is being planned and/or reviewed, each person in that particular PLC needs to come to an agreement of when, and for how long, each standard, goal, or skill will be taught. This does not mean that it cannot be changed or modified later, even on a week-by-week basis, so long as the team agrees on it as a whole. As stated already, the pacing guide should be considered a living document and will require modification and constant review. The reason for planning out each standard, goal, and skill is so that the PLC will be able to coordinate their common assessments in a logical and time-sensible manner. Two examples of this are demonstrated in the figures below.

Each figure outlines a fictitious timeline for a unit of study. Figure 3.1 demonstrates the use of initial and targeted instruction in a linear manner. In this example the entire class would receive the same initial instruction and, before moving on to any new material, the teacher and support staff would provide targeted instruction to all students and then reassess those who did not initially demonstrate proficiency. All of this would be done prior to moving on to any new material.

Figure 3.2 represents the same unit of study but highlights a cyclical approach to integrating targeted instruction. In this scenario, targeted instruction is integrated each day during a separate block of time that is buoyed by the assistance of support staff. As such, the targeted instructions for the previous standards occur during the same instructional days as the new instruction. Time can also be made to accommodate additional remediation and enrichment prior to a set of standards being assessed. This

Understanding the Process—Part 1

Unit 1										
Week 1		**Week 2**			**Week 3**			**Week 4**		
5 Days	1 Day	1 Day	2 Days	1 Day	4 Days	1 Day	1 Day	1 Day	2 Days	1 Day
Standards 1.1, 1.2		Quiz (1.1, 1.2)	Targeted instruction 1.1, 1.2	Re-quiz	Standards 1.3, 1.4, 2.1	Quiz (1.3, 1.4, 2.1)	Targeted instruction 1.3, 1.4, 2.1	Re-quiz	Unit Review Standards 1.2, 1.3, 1.4, 2.1	Unit Test

Figure 3.1 Unit Pacing—Integration of Linear Targeted Instruction.

Understanding the Process—Part 1

Unit 1

	Week 1	Week 2					Week 3					Week 4			
	Mon-Fri	Mon	Tues	Wed	Thurs	Fri	Mon	Tues	Wed	Thurs	Fri	Mon	Tues	Wed	Thurs-Fri
	Standards 1.1, 1.2		Quiz (1.1, 1.2)	Standards 1.3, 1.4, 2.1					Quiz (1.3, 1.4, 2.1)	Unit Review: Standards 1.1, 1.2, 1.3, 2.1				Unit Test	Introduce Unit 2
	Targeted Instruction (preventative maintenance) 1.1, 1.2			Targeted Instruction 1.1, 1.2		Re-quiz	Targeted Instruction (preventative maintenance) 1.3, 1.4, 2.1			Targeted Instruction 1.3, 1.4, 2.1		Re-quiz	Extra Unit Review		

Figure 3.2 Unit Pacing—Integration of Cyclical Targeted Instruction.

example can only be achieved if time is built into the master schedule to facilitate a targeted instruction block.

Common pacing guides are established in PLCs because it is only fair to both teachers and students that each class and each student is given the same opportunities for learning and that the education a child receives isn't dictated by what a teacher likes to teach most. Teachers need to be given an equal number of instructional days to teach, and student to learn, each skill, otherwise lessons may lack the needed focus and rigor that students need to be successful. We cannot teach one thing and assess something else, and teachers cannot be expected to plan and teach appropriately if they don't have a clear vision of the timeline they have available to teach each standard, goal, and skill. Also, the data garnished from common assessments may be artificially inflated or deflated based on the length of time one teacher had to teach a particular standard or unit compared to their peers. There's no way to measure and identify best practice if one teacher spends twice the time as their peers do on a particular standard.

During the pacing phase the PLC should begin grouping standards together, while paying special attention to those standards that need scaffolding. Instructional units should help break down and segment the pacing guide one standard at a time. Even though the goal is to break down the pacing guide to allow teachers to focus on, and then assess, one standard at a time, they may find that some standards just go together exceptionally well, or that they cannot teach one standard without logically including another. As I would tell my teachers, some standards go together like peanut butter and jelly, and it just makes sense to teach them together. Other times there literally isn't enough time to teach standards in isolation and there is no choice but to group standards together.

However, you should be very hesitant to include more than two or three standards in a single assessment that is not a unit test, benchmark, or end-of-year assessment as it would be difficult to appropriately analyze the data and provide a concentrated focus on exactly what skills or concepts students are lacking.

Assessment practices need to add value to our classroom and smaller, more frequent assessments enable teachers to provide timely and data-driven responses to student learning than do infrequent, larger assessments.

Mixing too many standards together also makes it difficult for teachers to identify exactly what was taught well versus what areas they may need to improve their instruction in and assist their students with.

Understanding the Process—Part 1

Unpacking Standards

Often times, in this process there is not nearly enough emphasis placed on unpacking standards. Lightly unpacking and discussing the standards will, and should, happen while reviewing the pacing guide. However, this should not be misunderstood as being a true and complete unpacking process. The unpacking of every standard does not need to occur at one time, nor would I recommend that you approach it in such a manner, due to both time restraints and the amount of information a single person can digest and retain at one given time.

Even though an in-depth unpacking may not have taken place prior to implementing PLCs, each team should be mostly content and knowledgeable in regards to the general curricular direction their pacing guide is taking them.

> The unpacking of standards will help to ensure that each PLC is accurately targeting and reflecting on the appropriate learning concepts.

The unpacking of standards will help to ensure that each PLC is accurately targeting and reflecting on the appropriate learning concepts, while also ensuring that teacher-made common assessments are properly focused. It doesn't matter how rich the conversation is or how we respond to our assessment data if the data we're responding to isn't accurately reporting student understanding of the concepts that are supposed to be learned.

If the unit standards have not already been fully unpacked prior to teaching the first standards or creating the first assessment, then the team must meet to discuss and unpack the standards in depth. The assistance of curricular support personnel can be quite advantageous when you first start this process. It is not necessary, but if you have the resources available at your school or if your district is large enough to provide the resources, they can make this process much easier. None of the assessments for this first instructional unit should be made prior to unpacking the standards. When you unpack a standard you should be identifying the concepts and skills in both the standard and indicators: this will assist the team by

21

Understanding the Process—Part 1

focusing them on the skills and concepts students need to be successful (Ainsworth, 2003).

It is often thought that unpacking standards is only for new teachers. While it is true that teachers new to the profession or new to a particular grade level or subject area surely need additional time to unpack their standards—which should be obvious as they have never taught the standards associated with their content—they are not the only ones. Experienced teachers who have taught for multiple years in the same grade or subject could also benefit greatly from taking the time to appropriately unpack their standards, especially if the curriculum has been updated during their tenure.

- Unpacking standards helps teachers to clarify and better understand their instructional intent while also assisting them to hone-in the rigor of their instructional tasks. Here are a few indicators that you or your teachers may benefit from taking additional time to unpack your standards. If there is little if any alignment between how well students do in class with how well they do on state exams or district benchmarks: On average, students receiving top marks in class should also be attaining the highest possible achievement level on benchmarks and end-of-year assessments. There should be an alignment between class performance and achievement level on these assessments. Have you ever asked yourself, "Why are my students making As and Bs in class and failing the end-of year assessment?" Or "Why aren't my students performing as well as they should be?" Or if a common excuse is "most of my students just don't test well." There are only two reasons for this: first, curricular alignment, or two, lack of appropriate rigor (indicators for this will be addressed in the common assessment section).
- You and other teachers at your school use good instructional strategies and it is evident that student learning is occurring, but it doesn't seem to translate to student success on state exams or district benchmarks.
- You know your kids can do it and you teach your heart out, but you just can't seem to get your students to where they need to be, even though they perform well in class.
- You just want to get the most bang for your buck.

Larry Ainsworth (2003) describes a simple and straightforward approach that teams can use to unpack or "unwrap" their standards in his book

Unwrapping the Standards: A Simple Process to Make Standards Manageable. Ainsworth states that teachers can separate standards and indicators into concepts by identifying nouns and noun phrases, while identifying the skills via the utilized verbs. The concepts are what the students must know, and the skills are what they must be able to do. Ainsworth provides multiple strategies, examples, and templates to aid in the unpacking process, and I highly recommend his book as a resource if your team, school, or district needs additional guidance in this arena.

Learning Targets and Alignment

After the team has agreed on the standard they will be teaching and has successfully unpacked the standard, they must align their learning targets for the standard or concept. Many teachers may frame their learning targets as essential questions, big ideas, "I can" statements, or some type of overarching statement or question that is visibly posted in their room and is utilized to provide a clear focus for their lesson.

Learning targets should be used to guide both teachers and students in a clear way that accurately directs their efforts toward the mastery of a specific goal or task and should be framed as "student friendly descriptions of what you intend students to learn or accomplish in a single lesson" (Moss & Brookhart, 2012). It is important that teachers proactively share their learning targets with their students. This allows students to purposely direct their efforts, set goals, and assess where they are and where they need to be. Learning targets are on course when both the teacher(s) and the student(s) are aware and aiming for the same goal (Moss & Brookhart, 2012). Learning targets should be referenced at both the start and end of a lesson, with possible periodic references throughout the lesson. They should never be something that a teacher writes or posts without making the students directly aware of their intent. Designing and sharing learning targets allows teachers to better plan and implement high-quality instruction by providing a clear and attainable goal that describes exactly what each lesson will teach. Using learning targets will also assist teachers in making informed and focused day-to-day and common assessments. This will guide their ability to appropriately differentiate and modify their instruction due to the frequency and focus of their assessment measures.

23

Understanding the Process—Part 1

The learning targets should remain focused on the skill(s) needed for the students to gain mastery of the particular standard and should be independent of whatever story or passages are being used to teach these skills. For example, if a teacher is using The Three Little Pigs to teach sequence, the learning target should not refer directly to the story, that is "List, in order form beginning to end, the four main events in The Three little Pigs." Writing learning targets in this manner is an extremely poor measurement of skill mastery, as it assesses student understanding of a story and not a skill. A student could simply memorize the order of events in The Three Little Pigs without ever grasping the concept of sequence. A better example of a learning target for sequence could be: "Explain why the sequence of events of a story are important." When worded in this manner the learning target still enables the teacher to utilize The Three Little Pigs, or any other short story/resource to teach sequence. However, the emphasis of the learning target is no longer on the story; rather it is where it belongs: on the skill. The teachers can now use multiple resources and activities without ever compromising the learning target or their instruction.

Remember that a particular standard or concept may have any number of learning targets and a new learning target is needed for each lesson. This does not mean that a teacher has to have a new learning target every day, as some lessons may take multiple days to teach. However, it is important to note that common learning targets do not have to translate into common lesson plans. Common assessments and common learning targets still allow teachers to have the freedom to utilize what they believe is best instructional practice, which will be vetted once the common assessment data is analyzed. Regardless of whether or not your team, school, or district chooses to use common lesson plans, the PLC process will remain unchanged.

Curriculum Guides

Curriculum guides are supposed to be just as the name implies: a guide to the curriculum. If the guide is correctly made and used, it can be an extremely valuable resource and can help guide and direct each PLC meeting. However, all too often these resources are improperly pieced together or not maintained and end up serving as nothing more than a space taker on a teacher's bookshelf. As a classroom teacher, I recall

24

referencing my curriculum two to three times a year. This wasn't because I didn't want to utilize it or because I thought I knew it all—truth was, it just wasn't a good resource. It in no way helped any teacher improve instruction, reach more kids, or provide insight to reach struggling learners. It didn't help teachers set academic goals for themselves or their students; and it was never talked about or referenced by any of the teacher leaders or administrators. It was simply a less-than-valuable resource and it wasn't until years later that one of my professors, Dr. Barbara Zwadyk, taught me the true purpose and power of curriculum guides and how perfectly they fit into the PLC process.

Before you start building a curriculum guide, you must first have a clear picture of what curriculum is. For this I will lean on Larry Ainsworth's (2010, p. 4) definition of curriculum: "the high-quality delivery system for ensuring that all students achieve the desired end—the attainment of their designated grade- or course-specific standards." Given this definition of curriculum I will move forward on the notion that a curriculum guide is simply "a guide for the high-quality delivery system for ensuring that all students achieve the desired end." This definition should make clear the intent of a curriculum guide as more than a definition of standards and pacing, while also providing a direct connection to the PLC process. Although it includes these things, the guide must also provide specific learning outcomes, research-based best teaching strategies for varying levels of learners, interventions, recommended resources, and assessments. This may sound like an impossible challenge for any school—which is why you must set an appropriate time frame that is integrated into the PLC process. Curriculum guides should not be viewed as separate entities when discussing student learning, instruction, assessments, and data, rather they should be front and center in this process and, as such, the center of each PLC meeting.

It takes about a year. Don't be shocked; what you just read wasn't a misprint. The process of identifying and recording best practices, remediation and interventions, recommended resources, and assessments that all properly and clearly align to the standards in both rigor and pace takes about a year—an academic year, to be more precise. And this is just for the initial documentation; the curriculum guide must be viewed as a living document that is flexible and committed to continuous teacher/student growth. It is when curriculum guides are viewed as "finished" that they will begin to lose their relevance and usefulness. These guides are never "finished," and if your school is operating proper PLCs it is easy to see why these are a vital and never ending part of the process that will help drive and focus teacher conversation and ultimately student learning.

> It is when curriculum guides are viewed as "finished" that they will begin to lose their relevance and usefulness.

There is no exact template that is going to fit the need of every school and every grade level, and there doesn't need to be so long as the same objective is meet. You may choose to utilize a different format with a different template from the one I am about to explain; however, the process and conversation should remain largely identical. Even if the template is done entirely digitally, the setup and organization will not change.

Step 1: Give each of your teams a one-inch binder for each marking period (four in a traditional setting). These should be labeled to accurately reflect the grade level (if applicable), subject area, and marking period that they represent, for example "3rd Grade Language Arts: First 9 weeks."

- Teams should not need a binder larger than one inch per marking period. If they do it is likely that there is too much "fluff and stuff." These are designed to be direct, to the point, and easy to use or flip through.

Step 2: The first page(s) in the binder should be the pacing guide for that marking period and the pacing guide for the entire academic year. This way, the team may always have a reference to the scaffolding approach for each of their standards. This will also give the team a clear picture of what needs to be completed by what time, so that the team can be sure to leave sufficient time to teach all the standards by the years' end.

Step 3: Insert some sort of divider directly after the pacing guide, and label it with the first unit and standard(s) to be taught, for example "Unit 1 standards 1.2 and 1.3." Immediately following the divider, place the template for the unit overview and the current standards (see Figure 3.3). These templates don't have to follow a specific format, but should, at least, include the sections shown in Figures 3.4 and 3.5.

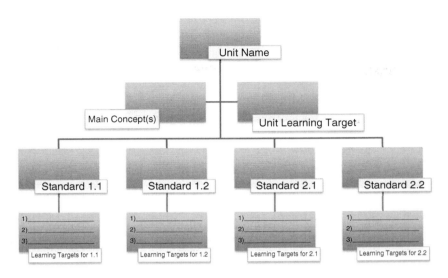

Figure 3.3 Unit Cover Sheet.

- As you progress through this process year-to-year, you may choose to add additional sections to your chosen template to "step it up," or to push school or district initiatives such as technological integrations, day-to-day common assessments that align with each learning target, targeted 21st century skills, vertical alignments, home and community involvement, and such like. However, don't start with too much too fast: keep it simple and thorough to start.
- Take notice that certain parts of this template will need to be filled out over multiple meetings. Before instruction actually begins for the selected standard, the team should fill out the suggested number of instructional days needed to teach the standard. Do not use actual dates as they can change from one year to the next; use instructional days, for example, five days. The standard should also be identified (column 1) as well as unpacked (column 2). Column 2 should include teachable concepts and skills and is essentially what the students need to know and be able to do (Ainsworth, 2010). Common learning targets, essential questions, and/or big ideas (column 2) should also be completed prior to the instruction for that standard, as should the academic vocabulary (column 5).
- Best practices and resources for core instruction (column 3) cannot and should not be filled in until after teachers have common assessment data

Understanding the Process—Part 1

(Grade/Subject/Unit)

Suggested time frame (Core) _____
Suggested time frame (Targeted) _____

Standard(s)	Learning outcome(s)/ Learning target(s)	Academic vocabulary	Best practices/Resources— Core instruction	Best practices/Resources— Targeted learning groups

Figure 3.4 Curriculum Guide Template (A).

Understanding the Process—Part 1

_____ (Grade/Subject/Unit)

Suggested time frame (Core) _____
Suggested time frame (Targeted) _____

Standard(s)	Learning outcomes, Learning targets, essential questions, or big ideas	Academic vocabulary

Best practices
Core instruction

Best practices
Targeted instruction

Figure 3.5 Curriculum Guide Template (B).

29

Understanding the Process—Part 1

to compare and analyze. There should be no guesswork for identifying best practices; this is one area where the data should rule. Once identified, best practices should be continuously refined and improved upon.

- Best practices and resources for targeted learning groups (column 4) should not be filled in until after the team has reassessment data to analyze and identify what practices generated the highest growth rates for students.

  - It is important to note that, for each of the best-practice columns, teams should never use descriptions such a "small group," "centers," or "differentiated instruction." These descriptors give very little usable information and fail to answer what strategy was actually used in the small group or how instruction was differentiated.

Step 4: Following the template, the team should record any resources that cannot be easily referenced on the template or that they deem as too important to ever risk losing (there generally should not be many, if any, resources in this section).

Step 5: Following the resources, place a copy of the common assessment and reassessment for the standard(s).

Step 6: Following the common assessments, teams should place a copy of their data sheets. This will drive year-to-year goal setting for the teachers for each standard, while also providing teachers new to each team or grade level an idea of what proficiency levels they will need to achieve in order to maintain consistent student performance and growth on end-of-year assessments.

Step 7: Following the data sheets, teams should place a divider and repeat steps three to six until the end of the marking period, at which time they should be given a new binder for the second marking period and the process should repeat itself.

- Using new binders for each marking period will keep the content to a manageable size that can be easily flipped through and sorted while also preserving the usable life of the curriculum guide by avoiding the unnecessary wear and tear that would come from using one binder for the entire year.

Regardless of what template you chose to use, at the end of the process you should have a resource that provides teachers with an exemplar that

30

they have created of what to teach, when to teach it, the best ways and resources to teach and remediate or enrich it, the assessments to test it, and a performance indicator to enable them to raise the bar and set personal goals. This guide will only become more focused and more refined year-to-year so long as the process remains in place. Also, since it is a living document and should be constantly revised and improved, it will never become outdated or irrelevant. Picture the power of this resource from the point of view of a first-year teacher, and ask yourself how much you would have appreciated a resource such as this when you first entered the classroom? How much more effective could you have been in impacting student learning?

Common Lesson Plans

Although there are many benefits to using common lesson plans, many educators may feel as though it encroaches on their creative freedom. It is not essential to utilize common lesson plans in order to get results from the PLC process. If your school or PLC is unsure of whether or not to utilize common lesson plans, I would simply suggest that you let your data be your guide. If the teachers are able to get good results and are accelerating student growth while using individual lesson plans, then they should be allowed to do so. Although, if current lesson plans are lacking in depth or rigor and you or the team feel as though there could be benefits from common lesson plans, then this approach should be pursued.

> let your data be your guide

There will be no guesswork when it comes to identifying high- and low-quality instruction in this process. When analyzing the common assessment data, teachers should be able to clearly identify the instructional strategies that were effective and those that were not. All members of the team need to remain open to improvement and change in their instructional and planning approach. Integrating best practice into one's lesson should never limit one's creative freedom. However, if one's creative freedom is not focused in its approach and is not yielding results in terms of student learning, then it may benefit from some more in-depth and structured planning. Again, this should be quite clear from the data.

Never assume that just because a classroom doesn't look or sound the way you think it should that learning isn't happening. The common assessment data will clearly inform the team what instructional techniques are most effective. At this point the team may want to do common lesson plans or at least plan together to ensure that they are all utilizing the most efficient approaches, or to strategically implement and analyze the effectiveness of different tasks and strategies. I simply recommend that you choose to do what works best for you. Just don't confuse common planning (essential for this process) with common lesson plans (not essential for this process).

Conclusion

You should now have a basic idea of the steps required to front-load a PLC prior to any instruction being given. Expecting to successfully conduct PLCs without any of the necessary front-loading would be akin to asking you to ride a bike without any pedals. It could be done with quite a bit of extra effort, but it would neither be efficient nor enjoyable, and you would likely find yourself better off walking. Or, in this case, teachers and schools would likely find themselves going back to their business-as-usual methods that found them failing to achieve the desired student and teacher growth in the first place.

References

Ainsworth, L. (2003). *Unwrapping the Standards: A Simple Process to Make Standards Manageable*. Englewood, CO: The Leadership and Learning Center.

Ainsworth, L. (2010). *Rigorous Curriculum Design: How to Create Curricular Units of Study that Align Standards, Instruction, and Assessment*. Englewood, CO: The Leadership and Learning Center.

Moss, C., & Brookhart, S. (2012). *Learning Targets: Helping Students Aim for Understanding in Today's Lesson.* Alexandria, VA: ASCD.

Reeves, D. (2010). *Standards, Assessment, and Accountability: Real Questions from Educators with Real Answers from Douglas B. Reeves, PhD.* Englewood, CO: The Leadership and Learning Center.

Understanding the Process—Part 2

Common Assessments

Common assessments are the focal point of PLCs; much like the sun is the center of our solar system, everything in the PLC process revolves around the common assessment. Common assessments are one of the most valuable tools for building teacher efficacy and capacity to improve. They are an excellent resource for determining how well the curriculum is being both taught and learned. When used properly they can help fuel amazing change in our professional practice by systematically offering a collective response to the learning needs of students (DuFour et al., 2010).

> everything in the PLC process revolves around the common assessment

The trouble that many teams and schools have is that they don't understand exactly how to use the data from common assessments and also don't understand the framework for successfully using those data. This chapter will attempt to simplify the most prevalent type of assessments used in PLCs—tests and quizzes—while providing some clear guidance to help put you on the road to success.

Understanding the Process—Part 2

Determining Proficiency

It is important that the staff agrees on a set proficiency mark prior to beginning any assessments. This is necessary in order to determine remedial and intervention needs. The proficiency level should signify the percentage or level at which teachers are confident that students have acquired the necessary skills and knowledge needed to proceed to the next standard and/or skill with confidence. Stated another way, you could ask yourself "Do I feel confident that my students 'get it' when they can score 70 percent or higher?" I would generally recommend that a school starts with the grade point average separating a C and a D, as a C is supposed to represent proficiency.

Schools may also elect to take a tier-based approach that includes three or four ranges. Tiers are helpful in identifying and categorizing students and appropriate interventions more explicitly. For example, students scoring 50 percent or below on a common assessment may be categorized for intensive remediation because they have a lack of understanding of the standard, goal, or skill. Students scoring between 51 percent and 70 percent may be slated for moderate remediation because they have some foundational understanding of the content. Students ranging from 71 percent to 85 percent may require some reinforcement and some mild acceleration, and those demonstrating mastery of the content, in the 86 percent to 100 percent bracket, may receive some accelerated projects/instruction because they have demonstrated continued proficiency and/or mastery.

Whether your school decides to implement a set proficiency mark or utilize the tier-based approach, it is important that all teams within the school operate on the same system: proficiency mark or tiers. This will assist in eliminating parental and student concerns that may arise from having different expectations from different grade levels or teachers. Parents and students may not be pleased if 3rd graders only need to receive a score of 70 percent to be proficient, but 2nd graders need to score 80 percent. Finding a consensus and operating on the same norms and common terms will assist in creating a shared vision, and aid in the understanding that the expectations are the same for everyone. This can usually be determined within about 15 to 20 minutes during a faculty meeting. Giving teachers time to consider this information prior to the meeting may also help to speed up the process.

If you are just starting this process, I would generally recommend you start with a single proficiency mark and that it should coincide with the grade-point average separating a C and a D, because, as I noted earlier,

35

a C is supposed to represent proficiency. The exact numeric percentage point for this will vary depending on whether your school uses a 7- or 10-point grading scale.

The whole purpose for establishing a proficiency mark or a tiered system is to provide each PLC with a clear indicator of student success and to assist them in identifying the level of remediation or enrichment that will benefit a student the most.

Planning Common Assessments

Any type of assessment can be a common assessment; however, this section will mainly be discussing assessments given normally as tests and quizzes. These assessment types will not be the only types of assessment data used during a PLC meeting, but they will be the most prevalent, especially when first starting the process. The purpose of these common assessments is to identify and measure student learning after the teacher has completed their initial instruction on the specific standards, goals, or skills. This should be no different than the existing process currently used by most teachers. Usually these assessments are multiple choice, short answer, or fill in the blank, but they can follow any preferred format.

Although the process may sound familiar and it likely mimics most normal test and quiz setups, the protocols are very different. Before continuing, it is important to note that there is no required testing format for this process to work effectively. These assessments can emulate any preferred format so long as they can be used to accurately measure student learning on various levels without the ambiguity of opinionated assessing that may come from grading a paper or project. There are, of course, exceptions to this, as a good grading rubric and/or team grading can often overcome subjectivity concerns. However, using these methods does require a steeper time investment.

Pacing guides and unpacking documents/protocols are an integral part of the common assessment process. Assuming that the pacing guide has been finished or at least outlined, it is time to identify the standards that are about to be taught. If you have not already done so, unpack the standards, as that must be done prior to making the assessment for it. The PLC should establish a time for the first common assessment to take place. This should be based on the number of instructional days the team believes they need to teach the specific concepts.

Understanding the Process—Part 2

When recording this in your curriculum guide, I recommend writing these in terms of instructional days (e.g. 5 instructional days) rather than dates (e.g. April 2nd – April 6th). This way, regardless of year-to-year calendar changes, field trips, or school cancelations, five instructional days will always mean the same thing. Whereas, if you plan and record by dates, you may forget that the length of time previously set was meant to accommodate any of the aforementioned inconsistencies.

Even if there are four or five standards in the instructional unit, each standard should still be planned one at a time whenever possible; this can usually be done each week as the team meets in their PLC. This will ensure a targeted and focused approach to both teaching and learning, and will provide a framework for efficient, concentrated, and targeted teaching and learning opportunities.

The length of time needed to teach each standard prior to administering the common assessment should be determined by the team and should be decided prior to the beginning of instruction for the particular standards they are about to start. Teachers should not feel obligated to assess only on Fridays. Although this is a habit among many educators, at some point they will either end up rushing a skill, concept, or standard, or dragging it out longer than necessary.

The common assessment needs to be completed and in the hands of all the teachers prior to the start of instructional planning for the skill or standard. Similar to what was discussed in the pacing guide section, teachers must know where they're going in order to be able to know how to get there. Having the assessment in hand prior to teaching will give each member of the team a clear idea and picture of what the students should be able to do in order to prove that they have attained the appropriate skill set by the end of the given instruction. This should not encourage teachers to teach to the test. It should, however, remove any potential ambiguity or confusion as to the exact purpose of the instruction the teacher is getting ready to deliver. Having the assessment in hand prior to teaching or planning will enable teachers to integrate similar and appropriate vocabulary, while also integrating appropriate instructional tasks, and integrating suitable ongoing or day-to-day instructional measurements that ensure the desired student learning is taking place. Without the common assessment in hand prior to the start of instructional planning, there is no way to appropriately plan without running the risk of teaching one skill and assessing another.

This is a critical first step for successful teaching and learning to be accurately measured, regardless of what level you work at. It is especially critical with younger students, who are in the first few years of their education, and still learning basic terms and vocabulary. One different word or term on the assessment that wasn't used in class can completely throw these students off as many of them are still too young to have attained the necessary critical thinking and conceptual skills needed to dissect text and identify or recognize innuendos. Teachers need to know what the common assessment is going to look like and what wording is used so that they may give their students comparable practice and familiarity in class. There is no point teaching one thing and assessing something else—or even giving the appearance of doing so—as it benefits no one. Be sure to teach what you're going to assess and assess what you taught.

Making Common Assessments

When teams first begin the PLC process, I recommend that they jointly make the first few common assessments together—this should not be debatable. This will give teachers an opportunity to learn and become familiar with what each member of the team values, while also giving them an opportunity to discuss and find appropriate rigor for the assessment. After the team gets on the same page, the task of making the common assessments can be delegated to a single member or a separate, smaller contingent of the team. However, the assessment still needs to be reviewed by the entire team prior to the beginning of instruction. This part of the process should never turn into one teacher simply handing out the assessment while everyone else simply accepts it without the opportunity to provide feedback. Regardless of how each PLC decides to logistically handle this part of the process, the opportunity for feedback and discussion is essential.

Having one person make these assessments prior to the meeting will leave more time for data and instructional discussion. Exactly how this is handled should be left up to each team to determine and will likely look a little different from team to team even within the same school. This process will also evolve over time, especially after the first instructional cycle when all the assessments will be used for the first time.

A thorough review of each assessment prior to instruction is a critical component of this process, especially when first starting. I continue

Understanding the Process—Part 2

to find it enlightening, and a little shocking, at the number of assessments I review that are completely focused on misaligned standards. Often these came from teams composed of veteran teachers whom I initially thought would have very little—if any—difficulty with the concept of "test what you teach." This error did not make these teachers bad educators; it simply speaks to the fact that so many educators are accustomed to doing things a particular way, and many have been doing so for 20 plus years with little or no guided feedback. Then, all of a sudden, they are being asked to rethink and revise their traditional assessment practices.

This process will likely present an interesting learning curve for those that have spent most of their career, and in many cases more than half their natural life, being assessed and assessing stories and books with a hodgepodge of varying and inconsistent standards. Asking them to shift their thinking to one that focuses on using a story or book to bring focus on a single standard can often be more difficult than it sounds. Some teachers will struggle with this, so remember to check for fidelity—that is, make sure it is being done right; be patient and understand that you are changing an unfortunate but consistent norm. However, do not confuse patience and understanding with the lowering of expectations: there is simply too much at stake for the acceptance of low expectations.

Length of Assessments

Teachers also need to be very cognizant of the length of these assessments. Since most assessments will only be assessing one or two standards at a time, there should be no need to have overly lengthy assessments. However, on the flipside, these assessments shouldn't be so short that a student risks missing the established proficiency mark by incorrectly answering one or two questions. In some subjects, such as calculus, a one- or two-question assessment may suffice, as the problems could be broken down into multiple sections in order to achieve the same grading principal as a traditional 15- to 20-item assessment.

Douglas Reeves (2010) advocates the use of frequent, very short assessments ranging from10 to 12 questions. He recommends that assessments be given on a weekly basis, but concedes that there are many successful models that function by assessing every other week. The key to successful assessments is not "simply doing the assessment," but rather

39

Understanding the Process—Part 2

using it to make immediate improvements to both teaching and learning. Timely, accurate, and specific feedback is the greatest influence on student learning. Reeves also warns that the longer the interval of time between assessments, the more difficult it will be for teachers to make meaningful changes to their instructional strategies and their curriculum.

Standards per Assessment

The number of standards per common assessment will vary largely between those counted as quizzes and those counted as tests. Although the goal should be to use quizzes to measure student learning one standard, goal, concept, or skill at a time, this may be logistically impossible or impractical due to time constraints or other variables such as logical scaffolding. Many grade levels can have 70 standards or more and creating a separate assessment for every standard is simply unrealistic. Reeves (2010) suggests narrowing the scope of the assessments and focusing on the key elements of the standards. Reeves also suggests that teachers identify the power or priority standards and place the majority of their emphasis on the standards that are most important.

As discussed earlier, it is permissible to give quizzes that contain more than one standard so long as the pairing is logical and beyond reproach. I have yet to see an example, where it made sense and was in the best interest of the students, to group more than two priority standards in one minor assessment. With that being said, I'm sure there may be some arbitrary example out there someone can point out. Just be sure to recognize that if this does occur it should be infrequent and is far from the norm.

There will also be cases where a standard may be too large to encompass in a single quiz. In these cases the team should divide the standard into key concepts and skills. This should be planned in advance in ensure that appropriate time can be spent solely on the particular standard without the need to integrate some smaller supporting standards into the unit. Although we operate on the undeniable premise that it is better to teach the content than it is to simply cover it, teachers must remain accountable for appropriately planning to teach all that they are responsible for.

The rational for the assessment limitation with quizzes lies in the data analysis and instructional reflection stage of this process, and also continues into the remediation and enrichment phases as well. When the PLC sits down to analyze its data, it is doing so in order to improve future instruction, as well as to plan how to reach those students whose initial learning needs were not meet, as evidenced by their inability to meet the established proficiency mark on the common assessment. In order to do this, teachers must be able to identify a precise instructional strategy or task that influenced a precise standard or learning target. This is an impossibility if too many standards are grouped together. Also, grouping too many standards together will result in overly large, and likely infrequent, assessments, or it will result in assessments that contain too few measurements per standard to accurately assess student learning of each standard.

On the other hand, tests used to assess an instructional unit will usually differ greatly from quizzes in both size and number of standards covered. Where the quiz should serve to test the various levels of the scaffold, the unit test should bring all these skills together and contain all of the standards from each of the quizzes associated with the unit. Although the range of these standards may be wide, its scope should still be focused and logical.

There is no mandatory number of major assessments that must be given in this process, unless prescribed by your district. However, you should have in the ballpark of no less than two and no more than five unit tests for every one benchmark given in a traditional calendar setting. This number may change from one marking period to another depending on the curricular demands of your pacing guide and the learning needs of the students.

Vetting Common Assessments

At this time you have probably already arrived at the conclusion that, since so much of this process depends on the common assessments, low-quality assessments would make this process a relatively pointless exercise. The question then begs to be asked: how can you be sure that you are using high-quality assessments without sending them off to be vetted or paying a consulting firm big money to come in and give you the okay? The good news is that there are a few simple guidelines that allow this process to be handled completely at the building level and they don't cost a thing.

The most difficult aspect of the whole vetting process is keeping an open mind and being reflective of the data. When analyzing assessment data it may be easy to give yourself a pat on the back if all the students of a team meet the proficiency mark or class averages are in the 90s. However, unless your school or team is normally a top performer in the district or state on the end-of-year assessments, it is not likely that the classroom grades are an actual reflection of the students' true achievement level in comparison with the state standards. If your common assessments are pulling scores in the upper echelon of the performance scale then you are literally saying, "Every one of my students are going to not just pass the coming benchmark or end-of year-assessment, but they are going to score in the top achievement levels on those assessments."

In addition to that, you are also saying that the teachers in the next grade level are going to be showering you with accolades for sending them an entire group of students who are all on or above grade level, and are so well prepared to face their next set of academic challenges. After reflecting on those points, you can determine if your scores do, in fact, earn you a pat on the back—or do they signify the need for more aligned and rigorous assessments.

So much of the vetting process revolves around internal assessment alignment. Within the same unit, the scores from the quizzes should roughly align with those of the unit test. If the class average, after remediation and reassessments have been given, of all the quizzes is 83 percent then the class average on the major assessment should be in line with this average. The closer to 83 percent, the closer both the alignment of rigor and standards are between the test and its corresponding quizzes. Some minor tweaking may be enough to improve alignment, but if all corresponding quiz and test averages are more than a letter grade apart from each (seven to ten numeric points, depending on your grading scale), then the assessment rigor and/or the standards are severely misaligned.

Logic should dictate that a corresponding alignment between tests and quizzes in no way signifies an alignment to state or district standards and expectations. It merely signifies an alignment at the school level, which is a necessary first step and should not be underestimated in its significance.

The most useful tools in aligning to state or district expectations is benchmark and end-of-year assessment data. However, if your benchmark assessments are not either district or state provided, then they will assist with little more than insuring school-based alignment. Hopefully, you also have the ability to itemize the benchmark results in order to identify strengths and weaknesses in the previous instruction. An item analysis will also help you to focus on specific assessments whose standards showed a lack of alignment. Without an item analysis, benchmarks are a relatively worthless measurement as they simply cover too large a swath of material to be effectively used to improve either alignment or instruction.

Conversely, if your benchmarks are district or state provided and they can be broken down by standard then you have an excellent tool to help assist with assessment alignment. Nearly the same approach that was taken to determine alignment between the major and minor assessments is used to determine alignment between the benchmarks and teacher-made assessments. Theoretically, the district, state, or other third-party vendor should have already vetted the questions on the benchmark assessment. How far and in what direction the major assessment average differs from the benchmark class average should give a rough idea of how well aligned the teacher-made assessments are with state and district expectations. If the benchmark can be itemized then each specific set of standards should be analyzed for alignment and adjusted as needed.

End-of-year assessments can also be used the same way. However, since scores for these assessments are not always released in a timely manner and states generally do not release an item analysis to teachers, their benefit can be limited. Couple that with the fact that these assessments only occur once per year makes it rather illogical to wait for them and base ones data-driven instruction solely on end-of-year assessment data.

Common Reassessments (Quizzes versus Tests)

Quizzes

Just as the initial assessments are given to target a specific standard, goal, or skill, so must the reassessment be specifically targeted. The purpose of reassessing students who did not meet the established proficiency mark is to provide an accurate measure that will determine student proficiency and academic growth after they have received remedial instruction, while also revealing the effectiveness of the remedial instruction.

Proficiency is great, but do not underestimate or undervalue student growth. Even when students initially fail to achieve proficiency, paying attention and responding to instructional strategies that yield growth is the only way to increase proficiency, as outlined in the scenario below.

43

> Proficiency is great, but do not underestimate or undervalue student growth.

A student named Joey takes the initial assessment on standard 1.1 and only responds to 20 percent of the content correctly. As a result of his low-content mastery, he receives mandatory remediation on standard 1.1 and then takes the reassessment. On the reassessment Joey responds to 60 percent of the content correctly. He may not have achieved proficiency, but there is still cause for celebration. Sure, he didn't make the cutoff, but he raised his content knowledge by 200 percent. As a result, the teacher should feel confident that the implored remedial strategy was effective, and the teacher should attempt to increase the time or frequency that Joey receives that specific remedial strategy. If Joey is systematically repeating this pattern, then the data should drive the teacher to begin to modify the core delivery of instruction to Joey in order to raise his competency after the initial core instruction. If the teacher can limit Joey's initial deficit, then Joey may be able to achieve proficiency after receiving the basic remedial services and eventually get to the point where he no longer needs consistent remediation.

In order to use one's data in this way, the PLC must ensure that both the assessment and reassessment are an "apples-to-apples" comparison. If the assessments are misaligned, they won't do Joey or any other student an ounce of good. To certify that this is the case, both the assessment and reassessment must be similar, if not identical, in length, rigor, and format. Do not make one test all multiple choice and the other all short answer or fill-in-the-blank. Each reassessment should contain the same number of question types, passages, and same number of questions per passage, whenever applicable.

Reassessments should be constructed at the same time as the initial assessment. This will help ensure continuity between assessments and should also ensure that each assessment has had the proper amount of attention and scrutiny while also making sure that everyone has appropriate

Understanding the Process—Part 2

time to plan their instructions accordingly. After each assessment is made, it should theoretically make no difference which one is assigned as the initial assessment and which is assigned as the remedial assessment, as they should both equally measure the same standard, goal, or skill.

Tests

The process for reassessing tests is quite different than that of quizzes. Unlike a quiz that focuses on only one specific standard, goal, concept, or skill at a time, a test may cover three or four standards. This makes the task of identifying exactly what each student was struggling with more arduous and time consuming. Also, a student could have fallen short of the proficiency mark, but may have excelled in one or more areas of the unit. As a result, remediating and reassessing the entire unit test would be time-consuming for both the teacher or the student.

There are a few recommended courses of action to pursue in regard to tests. The first, and likely the most preferred route if you are just starting out with this process, is not to do any type of formal reassessing with the major assessments. This is an easy argument to make, as teachers will already be extremely busy as they become accustomed to the PLC process and focus on student learning for each standard, goal, or skill. This is not to say that these assessments should be viewed as an autopsy that identifies a problem too late to do anything about it, or that the generated data should not be used to modify classroom instruction or to provide appropriate intervention for the students. I only advocate that the expectation for how these will be used is realistically established when you first start this process, and that teachers not be tasked with so much that can't properly manage and respond to all of their data. It is better to respond to a smaller amount of data properly than to inaccurately respond to a plethora of data.

Over time, once you and your staff have proficiently adapted to the PLC process, it will be easier to begin delving into the unit tests. These should be analyzed to monitor student growth for each standard spanning the length of the unit, as well as drawing correlations between classroom curricular and instructional demands, and those of the benchmarks and end-of-year assessments. When looking at the data you should be cognizant of any teacher or team patterns that may signify a need to review or revisit any particular standards, either in a small group or as a whole class. This is not guesswork;

45

Understanding the Process—Part 2

let the data tell you what needs to be done. Performing a simple item analysis on a unit test can also be used as a way to determine if continued remediation strategies were effective for a student or group of students.

The data from these assessments should also be used to provide further analysis of students in need of a Tier II or III intervention, or who may currently be struggling with an undiagnosed learning disability. Students who repeatedly fail to show adequate growth after receiving targeted core instruction, targeted and timely remediation, and targeted review of the scaffold material prior to a major assessment may be indicative of a missing or undeveloped foundational skill or a potential learning disability. However, a learning disability should not be assumed to be the problem and should never be the first stop to "fix" the problem. Utilizing a proper framework to assist these students, such as a Multi-Tiered System of Support (MTSS) or Response to Instruction (RTI), is necessary to identify if a student has a learning disability or is simply missing a core skill that is preventing their success on other performance goals.

Raising the Bar

As schools move through the data analysis process, they should find themselves constantly modifying instruction in order to better target the needs of their students. As a result of this data-driven approach to teaching and learning, schools should find fewer and fewer students in need of remedial services. This should come as no surprise since teachers will be collectively sharing data on a weekly basis and discussing the instructional techniques that lead to student success, or lack thereof.

On average, teachers should aim to have approximately 80 percent of their students meet proficiency after they have completed their core instruction and given their first common assessment. This goal is in line with Response to Intervention (RTI) and Multi-Tiered System of Support (MTSS) learning pyramids. However, more importantly, this target will ensure that a manageable number of students can be appropriately remediated, while also ensuring that the core instruction is appropriately geared for student success.

The percent of students who demonstrate proficiency can easily be artificially inflated or deflated by assigning an inappropriate proficiency cutoff score. As professionals, educators should be able to agree that it

46

serves no one's interest and proves nothing if the cutoff is unrealistically low, such as 50 percent. Remember, the point of the proficiency mark is to establish a cutoff between students who "get it" from those who don't and need extra help. When students are able to demonstrate mastery of 70 percent and 80 percent of the content, it is usually safe to state that they are proficient, and they "get it."

If the proficiency mark for your PLC is set at 77 percent, it is only logical to assume that over a period of time, say one to two years, the core instruction will improve and, on average, more and more students will consistently meet that proficiency mark. When, on average, PLCs have approximately 90 percent of their students achieving proficiency, I would recommend that it is time to raise the bar. Now, don't get carried away and don't be too conservative: this should not be guesswork; rather, it should be a data-driven decision.

Look at and analyze your data to find the appropriate target for your proficiency mark. This should be decided by determining where on the scale approximately 20 percent of your students would fall into the remediation group. It may only be a two- or three-point discrepancy, and it may seem too small to make a difference, but after a few years this can translate into some serious academic gains.

Conclusion

Common assessments are the cornerstone of successful PLCs. Any school claiming to hold PLC meetings without data-driven conversations derived from common assessments is not implementing PLCs and should not be surprised when their "PLC" yields no measurable benefit to student learning. Team-developed common assessments have such powerful implications that teachers should categorically not be allowed to opt out of them (DuFour et al., 2010). You cannot conduct a proper PLC without them, and you certainly can not claim to be operating a PLC if the focus is not orientated around them.

Remember that there is no specific way these assessments have to look or format they have to follow. However, if your team, school, or district decides to implement common assessments, just remember that their purpose is to assess student learning in a way that allows teachers to react to and target academic needs. I think that DuFour et al. (2010) state it best: "If all students are expected to demonstrate the same knowledge and skills regardless of the teacher to whom they are assigned, it only makes sense that teachers would work together to assess student learning."

The power of the process in this section should be a clear-cut and easy-to-follow guide to serve any school, in any location, on any level, regardless of socioeconomics, culture, current achievement levels, goals, or curriculum to increase student learning and teacher effectiveness.

References

DuFour, R., DuFour, R., Eaker, R., & Many, T. (2010). *Learning by Doing: A Handbook for Professional Learning Communities at Work.* Bloomington, IN: Solution Tree Press.

Reeves, D. (2010). *Standards, Assessment, and Accountability: Real Questions from Educators with Real Answers from Douglas B. Reeves, PhD.* Englewood, CO: The Leadership and Learning Center.

5 Understanding the Process—Part 3

Using the Data

This part of the process maps out the way the PLC actually effects instruction, the way it looks, when it takes place, who is involved, and how it is all supported by the data. There are still some specific foundational concerns that are critical to the PLC process discussed in this section. These deal entirely with answering one of DuFour et al.'s (2004) critical questions: "How do we respond when kids don't learn?"

A process or plan must be developed to address what will happen when students don't learn prior to giving the first common assessment. In addition, you need to establish criteria to identify students in need of additional support and the types of support that is needed. For example, are students missing foundational skills from previous grade levels that need more intensive support, or is the problem a simple misunderstanding that can be remedied with remediation and additional practice or exposure to the content? If you don't have a plan in place to respond to your data, you're going to be left sitting on your hands without ever addressing the entire reason for having a PLC—student learning.

In my experiences, it is in the part of this process where many well-intentioned PLCs falter. When common assessments fail to influence instruction, therefore making the data derived from them meaningless. Remember, to establish a new culture you must have a solid foundation to build upon and meaningful use of common assessment data is an integral part of that foundation.

> to establish a new culture you must have a solid foundation to build upon

Understanding the Process—Part 3

Using Common Assessment Data

It is well known that many educators are data rich but information poor. We collect an absolute plethora of student data, but utilize very little of it to its potential. The type of assessment data used and discussed in PLC meetings will vary from one context to another, but in most cases it is the team-made minor (quiz) and major (test) assessment data that will drive the majority of conversations. The rationale for this is quite logical: benchmarks and end-of-year assessments occur too infrequently to be consistently relevant when addressing the immediate needs of students to master grade-level standards. Individual teacher-made assessments are better suited to address immediate needs. However, these should occur with such frequency that meeting to discuss all of them is a logistical impossibility.

Much like Goldilocks had to find the bowl of porridge that was "just right," because the others were either too hot or too cold, we need to find the assessment tool that is just right for this process, and it tends to be the team-made minor and major common assessment. This allows teachers to support students along the learning path rather than waiting until a major assessment is given to see that students don't understand the material.

Too Cold

As previously stated, benchmarks and end-of-year assessments only capture a specific moment in time and that moment is usually void of teacher input as the dates and timelines for these assessments are typically determined at the state or local level—they're too cold. As a result, their relevance begins to fade soon after the teacher reviews student weaknesses or moves on to new standards. This is not to say that these assessments do not have their value, but if we sit around waiting until after these assessments to adapt our instruction to meet the needs of our students, we will be giving too little too late. Intervention, on all levels, needs to be an ongoing process, not one that occurs only a few times during the year.

Too Hot

Individual, teacher-made day-to-day informal assessments should occur with such frequency that it would make meeting to discuss these results

50

Understanding the Process—Part 3

a daily occurrence. By their very nature every lesson should contain at least one such assessment, often times more. These day-to-day assessments should be utilized by teachers to modify their instruction during the core instructional period, while also providing insights to modify their plans for the next day.

This is not to say that the data from these ongoing daily assessments can't drive a PLC meeting, and on occasion they may. However, for this to be the expected procedure, PLCs would have to meet on a daily basis to create high-quality common daily assessments, analyze the previous day's assessment data, appropriately group students, and have each support teacher and/or specialist respond appropriately to their targeted learning group. This would mean every person, every meeting, every day.

In a utopian setting, with more than 24 hours in a day where teachers receive more than the bare minimum planning allotments, this may be possible and would likely yield astounding results. However, all of the educators whom I have worked with live in a world with 24-hour days, and most already devote the vast majority of their waking hours to their students, making this route nearly impossible and quite impractical.

Just Right

So what makes team-made minor and major assessments just right? For many, this derives from using a tool with a familiar format that is easily assessable and provides clear data. I would imagine that all teachers and nearly all students are familiar with traditional tests and quizzes.

Other advantages that these assessments offer is time and ease of logistics. Every student in the class can easily be given the same assessment at the same time without the teacher needing to reinvent the wheel. The only thing some educators may need to learn is to modify the length of time these assessments are designed to take. Although the assessments should not be so short that a student cannot make a single mistake without qualifying themselves for unnecessary remediation, they also should not take the entire class period simply because that is what the teacher is accustomed to. Remember, when you are only assessing one standard at a time the need for overly long assessments becomes unnecessary.

Four-Letter Words

For some, the words "test" and "quiz" are just as bad as other four-letter expletives, and in many cases I would agree. When you don't use testing data to improve learning, the mere mention of them should be considered an expletive. Educators test and test, but traditionally rarely do much, if anything, with the data. Often assessment data is used to say, "I knew little Johnny would do well," or "Sam always struggles, so I'm not surprised by his performance...if only he would work harder..." All tests given during the school year should be used to modify and improve instruction in order to benefit students.

> When you don't use testing data to improve learning, the mere mention of them should be considered an expletive.

The conventional testing process throughout the school year looks much like the illustration in Figure 5.1.

Teachers deliver instruction and then give an assessment, prior to moving on to new material, which may or may not be scaffolded. Some common rationale for this is to hold students accountable, to teach them responsibility, or to make them earn their grades. When students don't do well, they are often given such sage advice as "do better next time," or "maybe if you did your homework you would have done better," or—the all-time favorite—"you need to study harder, this information *will* be on the test."

These assessments generally lead up to the unit test, which is often preceded by a one-day review of everything in the prior assessments. Throughout the whole process, all students generally receive the exact

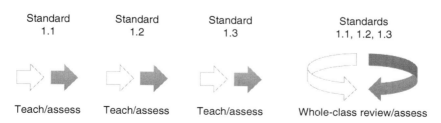

Figure 5.1 Traditional Assessment Illustration.

Understanding the Process—Part 3

same instruction and review, regardless of whether they need it or not. This process is repeated until the end of the year, at which time the teacher takes the last few weeks and tries to cram in a year-long review so their students can pass the final assessment.

Sound familiar? It should, this is the traditional testing method that many educators currently use and that most, if not all of us, went through as students... Given such a stellar approach to teaching and learning, it's hard to imagine why testing has gotten such a bad rap. (Please note the heavy sarcasm.) The truth is simple: a one-size-fits-all approach simply doesn't fit.

Teachers know, better than anyone else, that not all students enter the classroom with the same background knowledge. They know that not all students learn in the same way, and they are completely familiar with the knowledge that not all students learn at the same pace. I would place money on the fact that there is not a teacher, still employed, who would argue with that. So the question begs to be asked, why do we instruct and assess as if we didn't know that?

The first thing we must do is change the traditional assessment process from one that advocates the "just keep chugging" mentality to one that sees the entire year as a remediation and enrichment opportunity, as shown in Figure 5.2.

Notice that after each assessment there is an opportunity for students to be remediated and enriched *prior* the next assessment. This serves as a catalyst to provide teachers with the necessary framework to ensure they have a way to keep students from getting farther and farther behind. Teachers are immediately responding to the data before it's too late. This process trains and allows teachers to use assessment data while it is still relevant and to target specific student needs one standard at a time.

Remember that the number of instructional days needed to teach each standard, goal, and skill should be determined prior to the first day of instruction, and it should be up to the PLC to determine when it is appropriate to give an assessment. However, the number of days needed to teach a standard can always be modified based on need. This need should be derived from student performance on each teacher's ongoing daily assessments. Continued overall student performance on the day-to-day informal assessments should serve as a measure to each teacher whether the time frame for a particular standard, goal, or skill is actually appropriate. A teacher should never be "shocked" by their class results on a common major or minor assessment, assuming the teacher

Understanding the Process—Part 3

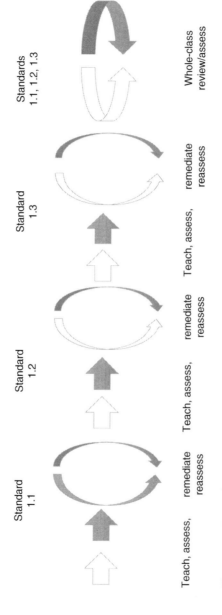

Figure 5.2 Revised Assessment Illustration.

is conducting frequent and high-quality day-to-day informal assessments throughout each lesson.

Make Time to Target Student Need

There must be time allocated on the master schedule to accommodate targeted student learning needs. This scheduled time may be called many things, but regardless of its name it should always serve the same purpose: to provide an opportunity for teachers to give focused instruction that remediates deficiencies, provides support for students to maintain and build upon their current level, or allows opportunities for students to receive enrichment. This is not something that can be properly addressed one day out of the week. Schools should try to schedule a daily block of time for this, if logistically possible.

Some schools that have either been unable or disinclined to tackle the logistical aspect of a daily targeted instruction block have found success integrating a couple of days after each common assessment to do targeted grade-level or content area instruction. This also takes a little logistical planning in regards to content pacing, but may be more attainable for middle and high schools that do block scheduling (see appendix for examples of elementary, middle, and high school schedules).

This targeted instructional time should be built to serve students across the learning spectrum. This should not be conducted as whole group or a one-size-fits-all approach. It is just as important to provide recognition to the varying groups that will be served as it is to recognize the fluid nature in which this system should operate. Students should be served in accordance with their achievement level, which could easily change on a week-to-week basis.

A targeted instruction block should be organized to provide remediation, intervention, maintenance, and enrichment opportunities to students. It is important to differentiate student needs so that each PLC may appropriately group students and successfully respond to their learning needs.

The remediation group should be set up to provide standard or concept remediation to students who were not proficient on grade-level standards or concepts as reported by a common assessment. These students may need the material presented in a different approach to reach proficiency or mastery. As with all the other groups of students receiving targeted instruction, educators need to be prepared to teach the way students learn and not expect students to learn the way the teacher teaches. Remediating the content by covering the same material the same way it was done during the core instruction, but making the delivery slower and louder, is not remediation and will not yield positive results (see Figure 5.3).

The purpose of the intervention group(s) is to review concepts and skills that were supposed to be acquired in previous grade levels. The lack of these skills is most likely hindering the students' success and will keep them from reaching proficiency regardless of extra remediation. This group of students does not need to be reassessed per the common assessment, but other measures should be put in place to monitor the success of the intervention they are receiving. Regardless of who is providing the targeted intervention, it should be research-based and its impact must be measureable (see Figure 5.4). In order to be truly successful, an intervention must provide students with assistance beginning with their most foundational skill deficit.

The maintenance group is usually the largest group of students. It is comprised of students who understand the process but may need additional

Figure 5.3 Remediation.

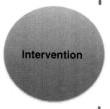

Figure 5.4 Intervention.

Understanding the Process—Part 3

differentiated practice in order to fortify their concept proficiency or move them to mastery. It is often plausible to align these students with the enrichment group utilizing either a problem- or project-based activity (see Figure 5.5).

The students in the enrichment group are usually the high flyers. These students understand the concept(s) and can easily make the necessary curricular connections. Activities for these students should strive to incorporate higher levels of Blooms taxonomy while providing additional exposure to grade-level content. Enrichment should be standard and/or concept focused, but should not include the introduction of the upcoming standards or concepts as this will simply result in these students being bored and unengaged in future lessons (see Figure 5.6).

The figure below pulls in all aspects of the grouping in a targeted intervention block. Regardless of what you decide to call your targeted intervention block or how exactly you decide to format it to best fit the needs of your school, you must be sure to provide a clear framework and set of expectations so that PLCs can work to appropriately meet the needs of all students (see Figure 5.7).

It is equally important that this blocked time works in conjunction with support personnel in order to provide teachers with the support

Figure 5.5 Maintenance.

Figure 5.6 Enhancement.

Understanding the Process—Part 3

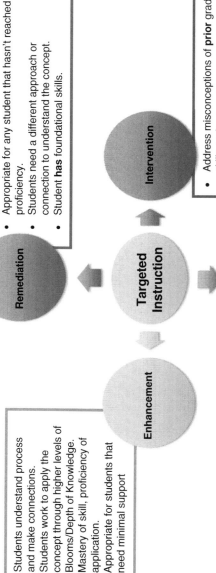

Figure 5.7 RIME Time.

Understanding the Process—Part 3

they need to provide meaningful experiences for all students. This is an important principle for scheduling committees, teams, or principals to keep in mind. Unless you work at a utopian school that has multiple support personnel attached to every grade or subject all day long, scheduling is key to success.

The reason for this is simple; a teacher may normally be tasked with providing instruction to 20 to 30 students, often more, on any given day in any given class. If that teacher is responsible for delivering a 90-minute block of instruction for Language Arts and then, later in the day, is given an additional 30-minute intervention block, how is the teacher supposed to provide a higher level or more targeted instruction than they already gave earlier in the day? It is highly unlikely that they will suitably serve all 20 to 30 students in a highly focused manner that provides necessary interventions to struggling students, provides high-quality work to help maintain proficiency, and provides enrichment for those higher flyers in a more meaningful way than they already have.

The reality is that without proper support one of two things will likely occur: either the targeted instruction time will look exactly like the normal classroom instruction with the classroom teacher providing whole-group instruction that is actually targeted toward those students needing remediation, or the teacher will pull out a small group of students who need remediation and the remainder of the class will be doing busywork.

Despite our best intentions, the work required of a teacher to provide consistent high-quality targeted instruction, in addition to their normal classroom instruction, without any additional support or collaboration would be extremely inconsistent. Sure, every school will likely have a few all-stars who stay up all night planning and making top-notch resources for their students, but this isn't fair or practical to expect. Most will end up doling out the busywork to the majority while they work with a small group. This isn't because they don't care or they don't want their students to grow, it's because most teachers are already so overwhelmed with curricular challenges, parent contacts, committee meetings, extra duties, and swath of other responsibilities that continually asking for more is just not realistic.

This is not a recommended practice born out of theory or hypotheticals, it is a practice born out of my own experiences and it is an experience that I want you to avoid.

59

Understanding the Process—Part 3

What It's Like without a Road Map

When I first implemented PLCs as a high-school administrator, it was right before school was starting and there was literally no time to revise or even consider changing the master schedule, and to be honest I don't recall ever even thinking about it. This error was mostly due to the fact that I didn't have a clear road map of how to do what I wanted. Despite all of my excitement and good intentions, what I actually ended up doing was giving the teachers a significant amount of extra data to look at but no way to appropriately respond to the data.

As a result of my lack of foresight, the PLCs had to create ways to work within the confines of a schedule that was not designed to accommodate a structured response to student data. Because of this, most teams were able to address and grow only a specific group of students. Progress was made with these students, but the mid- and high-level students were ignored. Without a block of time set aside to address student needs as indicated by the data, many teams began to rely on remedial homework packets; this proved mostly ineffective. I don't think anyone was surprised that students who didn't do the normal homework didn't do the remediation packets either.

Some teachers pulled out small groups of students while the rest of the class did something fun (and usually unrelated) or busywork (also usually lacking in focus). Some teachers tried doing small-group pull-outs while the rest of the class was working on material related to new instruction. As you can likely imagine, this only compounded the problem as these already struggling students were now missing new material and getting even further behind.

A few teachers who were lucky enough to have aligning class periods with other teachers that taught the same course were able to rotate students and pair groups of students with a specific teacher who would either work with high- or low-level students. However, this came at the cost of regular instruction and, without other support structures in place, the groups were often imbalanced and not nearly as effective as they could have been.

There was also a small set of teachers who had upper level or older students stay after school for a structured remediation. This worked only because all of those students were able to provide their own transportation. Although this after-school approach was successful for those struggling students, it still did not provide any enrichment opportunities to help grow students at all levels.

It should be understood that this process of intervention and remediation isn't just about helping a single group of students. It is about providing meaningful instruction to all students regardless of their ability level, and knowing how to use data to identify student learning needs while being able to respond appropriately to those needs.

Even without a proper framework our assessment data still reflected student growth. However, this process would have been much less stressful had we had a proper framework, and would have likely yielded higher results with less effort.

With a Road Map in Place

When serving as the administrator at an elementary school, and after having an opportunity to reflect and learn from previous issues that interfered with student learning. Our leadership team spent a large amount of time reorganizing and completely revising the master schedule with the goal of creating the best possible environment to support the process of data-driven student learning.

Each grade level was organized to have common planning times and common lesson times (3rd grade teachers taught arts at the same time and so on and so forth in all grades and all subjects). Every grade level also had a separate block of time scheduled throughout the day to provide targeted interventions. This enabled us to provide additional support to all of the grade levels during their blocked time with no overlap in service. We were able to support each grade level with a special education teacher, reading specialist, and teacher assistant. We also reserved the computer lab for each grade during this time so that students could have a structured time to utilize our learning software. Providing these supports allowed our teachers to focus their sole attention on a specific and manageable group of students. In order to pair each teacher with those students they could have the greatest impact on, the teachers could also trade students based on individual teacher results on the common assessments.

Just as at the previous school, our data showed that students' skills and competencies were growing. However, unlike the experience at the previous school, the process was easier and teachers were able to spend their

Understanding the Process—Part 3

time focusing on improving their instruction instead of spending countless hours figuring out how to manage more with less.

Instead of repeating mistakes that have already been made with solutions that have already been found, be sure to organize the master schedule in a way that gives your teachers an appropriate amount of time to focus on the data while also setting aside a time to respond to the data. This will take some time to plan, but the return on investment will be amazing. The goal should be to afford each grade level or subject area assistance from any instructional support staff. This will assist teachers and teams the needed personnel resources to specifically target the various learning levels in a highly focused manner.

Common planning times are a must, and common lesson times are also greatly advantageous in this process. The benefits to common planning times have been well researched and considered to be best practice since I entered the profession, and I have never encountered any resistance or opposition to common planning times.

However, it has been my experience that the advantages of common lesson times are rarely discussed or practiced. The benefit is that teachers are able to support all students by grouping them across the classes for specific activities, while at the same time more efficiently utilizing the support of teacher assistants. It is also a great boon for any administrator or instructional coach who is trying to grasp the instructional strategies and styles of each teacher. Ten minutes in the classroom during a lesson can easily give one a clear picture of how the instructional rigor of each class compares when everyone is teaching the same standard, measured by the same assessment, at the same time.

To better explain how this looks and differs from the business-as-usual approach, think about the current EC/ resource teachers at your school and what their schedule is. Chances are, unless you are that person, you don't know what their schedule is because they are all over the building pulling out students from different classes at different times in order to meet all the needs of their students' Individual Education Plans (IEPs). If your school has Math or Reading specialists, chances are that their schedules are equally as fragmented and as constantly changing as those of the Special Education teachers. It is also likely that, in order to serve their students, these specialists pull students out during the core instruction that students need in order to keep up academically with their peers, for example, providing extra Math assistance during the Reading block or visa versa.

62

Understanding the Process—Part 3

As stated earlier, it does struggling students no favor to miss new instruction in order to receive remedial or support services. All it does is ensure that these students will always need support services because they will always be getting their relevant instruction after their peers and after they've been assessed on something that they were never taught. Consistently pulling out students during core instruction is a great way to create a system of dependency and anticipated failure while demoralizing students in the process. I don't know about you, but that stands against everything I believe as an educator.

Now let's take a look at how each different support staff or specialist can influence your blocked intervention times and how an entire class can be broken down into manageable and targeted groups. Keep in mind that the resources at your school will quite likely differ from the example provided below; however, the process remains the same (see Figure 5.8).

This first example highlights how a school with ample support personnel can utilize their specialists to provide intensive interventions. While a teacher assistant takes a large group of students to the computer lab to work with an aligned computer-based learning program, the three remaining classroom teachers divide out the remaining students into remediation and enrichment groups (see Figure 5.9).

The second example highlights a school without the luxury of support personnel. In this case the resource teacher still provides intervention support to those students with special learning needs. However, the classroom teachers assist in serving students in need of both intervention and/or remediation. During the PLC meeting the teachers also compose activities

Personnel	76 Total Students	Purpose
Reading Specialist	5	Intervention
Math Specialist	5	Intervention
Resource Teacher	5	Intervention
Teacher Assistant	25	Maintenance
Classroom Teachers (x3)	12 each	Remediation/Enrichment

Figure 5.8 Breakdown of Targeted Instruction Supports.

Personnel	76 Total Students	Purpose
Resource Teacher	5	Intervention
Teacher Assistants (x3)	15 each	Maintenance/Enrichment
Classroom Teacher (x3)	8 each	Intervention/Remediation

Figure 5.9 Breakdown of Targeted Instruction Supports.

Understanding the Process—Part 3

and lessons with the teacher assistants to provide students with aligned maintenance and enrichment opportunities.

Remember, if your classroom teachers are not given structures and supports to appropriately target student learning needs then it would be impractical to expect better results. Administrators should do their best to provide additional student supports that specifically allow the classroom teachers the opportunity and environment to provide appropriate remedial opportunities to the students.

Scheduling for Students with Special Needs

The intervention time is a critical juncture for both teachers and students. Both teacher success and student achievement are intertwined and follow a common thread. Therefore, organizing specific teachers around this block of time will better serve all parties involved. Whether you are a teacher or administrator you know that some of the highest need students in a classroom are those who receive Exceptional Children services. It is at this time that these students must receive some of their allotted service. The rational for this is two-fold. First, it is the Special Education and resource teachers who should be the most qualified and knowledgeable regarding the needs of these students and the strategies that work best for them. So it only makes sense that, during that time of the day specifically blocked to serve as the targeted intervention time, these students also receive service from the person most qualified to serve them. If this does not already happen, then a fluent and regular dialog will need to open between the two teachers. Some joint planning and sharing of lesson plans should occur between the regular classroom teacher and the Special Education or resource teacher. This way the Special Education or resource teacher can more appropriately plan and target those remedial skills and foundations that support the current standard, goal, or skill being taught in the regular classroom setting.

The second reason is that students receiving Special Education or resource services tend to require a disproportionate amount of a teacher's time. This should come as no surprise since these students are already receiving additional services outside of the regular classroom in order to combat learning difficulties. Providing this additional Special Education or resource support during this time will allow teachers to better serve the

Understanding the Process—Part 3

other students in the class without compromising the needs of the students receiving special services.

One concern of scheduling in this manner, from a Special Education perspective, is that specific student accommodations that are stated in each Individual Education Plan (IEP) must, legally, be met. Not meeting these accommodations is a good way to get yourself in some serious trouble with your supervisors, cause some unwanted lawsuits, and might even cost you your job. One must remember that an appropriately written IEP is put in place to provide the necessary services in order to help a student to be successful. Shortchanging these students is not an option. The good news is that following this process of scheduling may not only help your schools meet the current IEP needs, but in many cases will help them exceed it.

> My school had two Special Education teachers who provided instructional support to students outside that were outside of the self-contained setting. One of these teachers worked with all of the students in Math at each grade level during the targeted intervention time. The school had three classes per grade with inclusion students equally distributed among each teacher on the grade level. For 30 minutes the resource teacher would pull all students into one classroom and work with them in building and reinforcing the foundational skills for each of the current standard being addressed in class.
>
> The other resource teacher would work with all inclusion students with disabilities in Language Arts. Since many of these students had disabilities in both Reading and Math, this teacher would go to each grade-level during their guided reading time. This 30-minute block was staggered the same as the targeted intervention time across the schedule to avoid conflicting grade-level needs and overlaps. Other schools may refer to this block of time as close reading time, structured reading time, literature circles, or focused reading time.

Splitting up and organizing the schedules in this manner will provided all of your inclusion and resource students with a minimum of five hours of intervention time per week. In addition to this, each of these teachers will have about two hours left in the day (not counting lunch) that they could use to "push in" to different classrooms, providing additional academic support to students with learning disabilities in a classroom setting. This will support both the classroom teachers and students with extra in-class support. This additional time can also be used to provide additional services to the few outliers whose IEPs required intervention time in addition to five hours per week.

This is not necessarily a one-size-fits-all approach and, in some cases, it may not fit the needs of a particular school or that of a particular student. Also, please note that this scheduling technique was used at a traditional elementary school serving grades kindergarten to grade five, and those working a different settings (i.e. non-traditional and secondary) may have to create their own adaptations that best serve their school and students. Each and every school has its own particular resources and unique challenges that contribute to the development of the master schedule, making it impossible for me to tell you or give you an example of exactly what to do at your school.

How Does Grading Work?

It can often be a controversial issue of exactly how to grade the assessments and reassessments. Do you count both? Only take the highest grade? Weigh the assessments differently? Before deciding how to grade the assessments, you must first determine the purpose of giving an assessment. Under this process the answer should be something along the lines of "to measure student learning, and to gauge the effectiveness of the given instruction and/ or intervention." There are really only two viable options that allow this to accurately and easily take place.

Option 1: Some may argue and provide rational advice for giving a student the higher of the two grades. For example, if Joey takes a quiz in class and scores 70 percent, then receives remediation and retakes the quiz and scores 80 percent, then many advocates would recommend giving Joey the higher of the two. In theory this sounds like a good idea; he did, after all, master 80 percent of the content and his grade should reflect his knowledge.

Pros: A student's grade reflects their current knowledge or mastery of the content.

Cons: Students may not try as hard or put the same effort into the first assessment if they know it doesn't count.

Understanding the Process—Part 3

Option 2: Others may recommend and provide rational advice for taking the average of the two grades. In this case, Joey takes a quiz in class a scores 70 percent, then after receiving remediation on the content he retests and scores 80 percent, Joey should then receive 75 percent in the grade book. However, if the determined proficiency for the school is 77 percent, then Joey's grade should be bumped up to 77 percent to reflect proficiency. This will accurately communicate Joey's proficiency to his parents and his future teachers. However, if Joey received a lower mark on the second assessment than he received on the first assessment, his grade should not be lowered and the grade book should reflect the higher of the two, as the processes within this framework should never create a situation that would intentionally demoralize or disenfranchise a student. This will provide students with a little extra incentive to achieve proficiency while not completely dismissing their effort on the first assessment.

Pros: Encourages students to put forth their best effort on the first assessment while reflecting proficiency for those students who make or surpass the mark.

Cons: Does not accurately reflect students current knowledge of the content.

The pros and cons of these two options may still not provide you with a concrete answer as to what method will work best for your school, so I will provide you a real-life example from my experiences that will hopefully help you avoid future difficulties.

> When I first began this process, I mandated that all teachers follow the guidelines of Option two. However, as will likely be the case, not all teachers in the school agreed with my selection. One department in particular felt very strongly that their students should receive the higher of the two grades. They were unified in their belief, and they knew that they could openly share their differing opinion with me without any fear of administrative backlash. After a relatively brief discussion of weighing the pros and cons of each option, I allowed them to begin the process under the guidelines of Option 1, even though the rest of the school was operating under the guidelines of Option 2.

There was only one stipulation I gave this department. They had to operate under the grading guidelines of Option 1 for the whole academic quarter. At the end of the quarter we agreed to reconvene and discuss how the process worked. Regardless of our differing options on the matter, we agreed that in the end we would let the data guide our decision-making. If their method yielded positive results, on par with the rest of the school, then they would be allowed to continue using Option 1, and if it yielded better than average results than the other departments then we would discuss restructuring the other departments, and possibly the rest of the school. However, if the results were not up to par then they would conform to the grading guidelines in Option 2.

As an educational leader, I had to remind myself to be open minded in this situation, especially because at the time the process was as new to me as it was to them. Also, I have always felt it is important for the teachers to have a say in new processes, especially those that they play such a significant role in. Besides, I didn't have any data to prove that their idea wouldn't yield positive results. So the mini experiment began—and soon ended.

We didn't even make it halfway through the first quarter when, during their weekly PLC meeting, the team was literally pleading to be allowed to switch over to Option 2. You see, their data was crystal clear, they had such a high numbers of students in need of remediation every week that they could not sufficiently assist them all. When directly asked, many of these students had no problem reporting the reason for their poor performance—they simply didn't try because they knew the first grade didn't count. This hurt our teachers and students on both ends of the process. First, more students were failing to learn from the initial instruction because they no longer felt accountable. Second, the teachers had such large groups of students in need of remediation that they literally didn't have the time or ability to provide proper interventions to those students who could have truly benefited from it.

Understanding the Process—Part 3

About two weeks after the department changed their grading process, it was as if someone had waved a magic wand and the first-round assessment data was on par with the other departments. For my teachers and me, this example wasn't a lesson about being right or wrong. It was about being open minded to differing views but, in the end, regardless of one's personal opinion, it was about doing what the data told us was in the best interest of our students.

I can't tell you what option will work best for your school or district, but I can tell you that I have never received a serious parent or student complaint (outside of general discussion) when using Option 2. Much of this may be in how it is presented. After all, giving every student who doesn't meet proficiency the opportunity to raise his or her grade sounds pretty good, especially since this wasn't even an option before. Also, if you firmly believe that a student's grade should always accurately reflect their current knowledge, as in Option 1, then technically every time a student receives an assessment on a current standard via tests, quizzes, benchmarks, or end-of-year assessments, then all of their grades should be fluidly changed to reflect the latest assessment data regardless of when or what quarter it takes place in. This is not a logistical can-of-worms I would ever want to open. Besides, I have met too many students who would likely slack off the entire year in hopes of doing well on the end-of-year assessment. As an educator this is simply not a risk I would be willing to take with a student's future, nor would I be willing to provide a structure that encourages this type of risk taking. To state it plainly, "students tend to take seriously only that work for which they are held accountable" (Doyle, 1983).

With that being said, I know many administrators—mostly at the elementary level—who successfully use Option 1 with little or no issue. These administrators included their staff in the decision-making process and were in tune with their school cultures enough to know that they wouldn't encounter many issues with student effort. When deciding what option is best for your building, know your school culture, know your staff, and include them to achieve a building-wide consensus.

> Know your school culture, know your staff, and include them to achieve a building-wide consensus.

What Students Are Reassessed?

When students do not meet the proficiency standard, they should automatically receive non-optional remedial instruction and assistance that supports their academic growth. After a set period of time, established by the PLC, these students should receive a reassessment on whatever standard, goal, or skill they were not proficient on. For these students this should not be optional.

Since these students lack the required proficiency, it should be evident that they do not have the skills or knowledge necessary to build a solid foundation. Without providing these students with a way to demonstrate proficiency, growth, or lack thereof, teachers will be ill equipped to provide data-driven instructional techniques that focus on each individual learner. This is why the remediation and reassessment process is mandatory for all students not achieving proficiency, regardless of a student's age or grade level.

Can students who meet proficiency be reassessed? The short answer is "yes"; however, these students should never be required to do so. Rather, they should be given the option to reassess only if they wish to raise their grade. I have seen and heard of numerous PLCs that reassess entire classes regardless of each student's achievement level on the initial assessment. This is a nonsensical approach that is born out of noting more than one's unwillingness to spend the time on basic logistics. There is absolutely no point in requiring a student who has already proved mastery of the content to take a reassessment. This will do nothing more than raise the ire of these students while teaching them that there is no reward for high performance.

How Are Students Reassessed?

The time and place of the reassessments should be determined by the PLC, and will likely be dependent on a school's space and resources. If a school is fortunate enough to have a staffed tutoring or remediation center, then this could be an ideal setting. If your school is similar to those that I have worked in and you do not have the luxury of a staffed tutoring center, then I would recommend that students take their reassessment during their

Understanding the Process—Part 3

targeted learning time, and that they take the reassessment in whatever room and by whichever teacher has been providing their remedial instruction. This way the process won't interfere with the normal classroom instruction or enrichment that other students may be receiving during this time. It is also important to note that this remediation and reassessment process should never be punitive, so keeping a student out of electives such as Gym, Art, or Music, or from recess should not be considered as appropriate to conduct either remediation or reassessment.

Regardless of the location of the reassessment it should be scheduled to take place after the initial assessment, but prior to the following assessment on a new standard. For example, if a teacher assesses standard 1.1 and then plans to assess standard 1.2 the following week, those students needing remediation on standard 1.1 should be given their remediation and reassessment prior to being assessed on 1.2.

Doing this ensures that teachers provide timely interventions and grow student deficiencies prior to those deficiencies producing a systemic model of expected failure. Why provide new instruction and assess new standards when a student is lacking the foundational skills necessary to be successful? Also, by completing the remediation process prior to giving the next assessment, teachers should have time to provide extra support during their targeted learning time to those students they know are struggling and have shown mixed or poor results on the daily informal assessments. Two examples of this are illustrated in Chapter 3, see Figures 3.1 and 3.2.

Minimum Grading Policy

It is likely that your district has some rule in place stating that students cannot receive a final grade below a certain level. For the sake of discussion, we will say this mandated minimum grade is 60 percent. Many schools or teachers operating in districts with grading practices such as this will still give students a whole range of grades during the year and will only raise the overall grade just prior to issuing a report card. They do what the district prescribed, but to what purpose? The students whom this is meant to assist still feel like a failure the entire year and have no hope of passing. Even if the student got on the straight and narrow midway through the semester, it is still usually impossible for them to pull their average above the mandated minimum. What would even motivate a student to try when failure is inevitable? Would you try given the same situation?

Minimum grading policies can work to motivate students that may otherwise become disenfranchised with education and give up (Guskey, 2004; Wormeli, 2006). Minimum grading policies are based on solid educational and psychological theory and are easy to implement (Carifio & Carey, 2012). Assigning even a low number of catastrophically low grades to a student early in a marking period can create a sense of helplessness that will likely become a foundation of systemic failure (Carifio & Carey, 2012).

The bottom line is that even if your district has a minimum grading policy established, it is most likely the equivalent of an F. And if the student decides to do nothing all year or all semester he or she will fail regardless of whether you put a 0 or a 60 in the grade book. However, if you can help motivate your student or they become intrinsically motivated then there is a reason for them to put forth the effort. No educator should be the one to stamp out the light at the end of the tunnel.

Conclusion

In order to provide your PLCs with the greatest potential to influence student learning you must provide a solid foundation from which to build. You must create a plan and expectation for how common assessment data will be used. You must also build a schedule that focuses on student learning and coordinates all school resources. You must also discuss and decide how reassessments will fit into the schedule, as well as the grading policy. These are all concerns that must be thoroughly addressed in order to answer the critical question posed by DuFour et al.'s (2004): "How do we respond when kids don't learn?"

References

Carifio, J., & Carey, T. (2012). The arguments and data in favor of minimum grading. *Mid-Western Educational Researcher, 25*(4).

Doyle, W. (1983). Academic Work. *Review of Educational Research. 53*(2), 159–199.

Understanding the Process—Part 3

DuFour, R., DuFour, R., Eaker, R., & Karhanek, G. (2004). *Whatever It Takes, How Professional Learning Communities Respond When Kids Don't Learn*. Bloomington, IN: Solution Tree Press.

Guskey, T. R. (2004). 0 alternatives. *Principal Leadership: High School Edition, 5*(2), 49–53.

Wormeli, R. (2006). *Fair Isn't Always Equal: Assessing and Grading in the Differentiated Classroom*. Portland, ME: Stenhouse.

6 Guiding the Conversation

Introduction

Our time is finite. As a result of this simple truth, you need to ensure that your PLC's meeting time is as productive as possible. I have seen far too many meetings start with the best of intentions and slowly deviate from their true purpose until becoming not much more than a casual conversation with little or no focus. This usually occurs when the waypoints needed to reach the final destination are murky and out of sequence.

This chapter will proceed on the premise that your PLC has a coherent pacing guide to follow and that the foundational steps discussed in the previous chapters have been discussed and addressed. If your PLC does not have a useful pacing guide then the formation of such would need to be completed in a different forum, as it would likely consume the entire PLC meeting, rendering its capacity to help teachers respond to student learning inert. It should also be noted that the sequence in this chapter revolves around the pattern that most meetings will follow when using team-made minor and major common assessments. Exceptions to this may include benchmarks, end-of-year, and other state- or district-level assessments.

The First Meeting

The first meeting of the year always sounds a little different than the following ones. This is simply because there is no previous team-made common assessment data to discuss. Theoretically, this meeting should be the briefest of all PLC meeting because it has the shortest agenda; however, if this is the team's first true PLC meeting it could easily take much longer than you initially expect. This isn't necessarily a bad sign and may simply be a measure of previous instructional collaboration.

After the team has established its norms, the first step in this meeting is to determine the instructional unit and the standards that will make up that unit. This should not be extremely time consuming, as the pacing guide should already outline an approximate path to follow. Once the instructional unit is determined the standards in that unit should be appropriately organized to reflect a logical scaffolding approach. The first standard in the unit should be read out loud and its unpacking documents reviewed to ensure that everyone is on the same page and is proceeding on common ground.

Now that the standard has been identified and reviewed, it is time for the team to make the first common assessment and reassessment (refer to Chapter 4 for additional details on common assessments). These common assessments should now be used to guide the team's learning targets or essential questions. Using common learning targets will ensure that all members of the team remain focused and that their instruction remains on task. Common learning targets do not necessarily have to mean common lesson plans or even common resources so long as the learning targets focus on each specific skill instead of a specific story or resource. Ensuring that each learning target is skill focused will still enable teachers to instruct with their own creative freedom while also ensuring that each learning target is appropriately focused on the targeted skill and not a specific story or resource.

The final step in this first meeting is to determine how the team will utilize its targeted learning time. Since there is not a common team-made assessment for which to provide targeted interventions, teams must decide how to best utilize this time. There are, as always, a few options. The first is to utilize this block of time to create the class norms and set expectations such as hallway behavior, bathroom protocol, classroom expectations, student contracts, and such like (see Figure 6.1). However, depending on the grade level the team may not need all this time to tend to protocols and expectations. In these cases I would recommend using your daily informal assessment data, previous end-of-year assessments, or pre-assessment data to provide additional support to those students you notice struggling at the start of the year. This should also help to boost the number of students meeting proficiency on the first assessment, which will pay dividends by providing teachers with manageable intervention groups while increasing

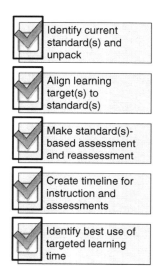

Figure 6.1   First Meeting Agenda.

the confidence of some students who may not always start with a successful grade.

The Second Meeting

The second meeting should begin the process for the best professional development your teachers have ever received. It is during this meeting that the true benefit of a PLC should begin to show itself. This is where the data first begins to drive instruction and educators can truly begin to springboard their success from one another. It is a powerful process that has limitless growth potential. However, do not expect each PLC to have a completely fluid experience from the start.

Now that the team has common assessment data to view and discuss, the second meeting has a different approach than the first. In this meeting the team will start with the data from the first team-made common assessment. The data needs to be displayed in a manner that is easy to view for all, and allows each member of the team to provide relevant feedback. A few possible templates are listed in the Appendix.

The meeting should begin with everyone receiving a copy of each other's scores (unless they have already been compi ed and are in hand). Some teams may choose to compile this data during the meeting, which

Guiding the Conversation

is a possibility—however, it can take valuable time away from the other aspects of the meeting. As a result it is recommended that the data be compiled into its preferred format outside of the scheduled meeting times.

> The goal is to identify best instructional practices, strategies, tasks, and resources.

After everyone has the data, it is time to begin some very purposeful conversation. Remember that the goal is to identify best instructional practices, strategies, tasks, and resources. Those team members with the highest achievement scores should be directly asked and should be equally willing to share what they did and how they approached their lessons. This isn't to say that others on the team won't have additional feedback to give and recommendations to improve those strategies and techniques even more. Just because a particular teacher didn't have the highest scores or proficiency rates doesn't mean that there weren't significant components of instruction happening that everyone may be able to benefit from.

I strongly recommend that teachers bring their lesson plans to these meetings so that they can easily reference their instructional strategies, and also so that they can make editorial notes regarding changes they want or need to make in order to improve their instruction and the student learning in their classrooms.

> If teachers in the PLC are at first hesitant to share and are protective of their data, or if sharing their data makes them feel exposed and/or defensive, then one of the educational leaders (i.e. administrators and/or curriculum coaches) should help the team ease into the sharing process by asking leading questions such as: "Ms. Smith, I see you did an excellent job working with your students. What techniques did you use that helped you communicate the information so well?" A different approach could be, "Why don't we start by having everyone share one thing they thought went especially well when working through this standard," and "If you could redo or modify any part of your instruction, what would it be?"

Guiding the Conversation

> An effective leader can help take this process to its highest potential, while an ineffective leader can absolutely destroy it.

I cannot adequately express the importance of quality leadership at this point. An effective leader can help take this process to its highest potential, while an ineffective leader can absolutely destroy it. As an educational leader it is vital that you convey, and help to establish and maintain, a non-threating environment that is inclusive and respectful of all members of the team. The team needs to know that they can openly respond to and share with one another in a supportive environment that is free of fear and possible administrative reprisals. By there very nature, these meetings will have teachers sharing both their successes and their failures: the latter can be a difficult thing to do. I would always share with my teachers, "This is not about you and it's not about me. It is about doing what's best for the kids." It shouldn't matter where a teacher is starting at, or how high or low their scores are. What matters is what they're going to do about it, and the growth that they are going to attain. I would rather have a team of mediocre teachers who were willing to grow and learn than a team of good teachers who refused to change. Because given a little bit of time and proper opportunities, the first group will soon catch and surpass the other.

After the data has been shared and the best instructional strategies added to the curriculum guide, it is time to discuss the team's approach to reach each of the targeted learning groups while deciding the composition of each group. The student composition of each group should generally be a fairly simple process, as it is data driven. The number of student groups normally depends on the available number of teachers on the team and available support staff. Examples of this are shown in Chapter 5, Figures 5.8 and 5.9.

Assigning teachers to the various student groups should be conducted much the same way that students were selected for each group. Whichever teacher in the PLC had the highest competency should likely be the one who conducts the remedial group, as those students are in the most need of great instruction. Likewise, whichever teacher did the best with their academically gifted students would likely be the best fit for providing academic enrichment to those high-level learners (enrichment should still be targeted on the specific standard, not just an arbitrary assignment or project). Support staff such as reading specialists and resource teachers should use this time to serve students in need of their specialized services.

Now that the assessment data has been analyzed, the best practices have been integrated into both lesson plans and curriculum guides, and both teachers and students have been placed into the targeted instructional group that they are most needed in, it is time to begin planning the team-made common assessment and reassessment for the next standard, goal, or skill in the instructional unit. Just as in the previous meeting, these assessments need to be completed and in the hands of all teachers in the team prior to the start of instruction, and ideally prior to the start of the planning for the instruction. After the assessments are completed the team should

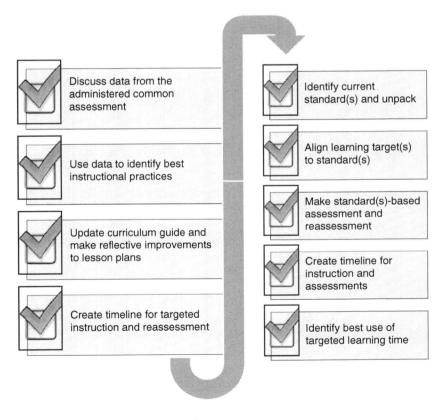

Figure 6.2 Second Meeting Agenda.

map out the learning targets that will be needed to bring the instruction for the targeted standard, goal, or skill to a final culmination (See Figure 6.2).

The Third Meeting

The third meeting marks the final step to the ongoing process; it is after this point that the process continuously repeats. It is in this meeting that the team will hopefully be able to identify student growth and begin to see the fruits of their labor. The reassessment data from the first assessment should now be available for review and is an additional piece of data to be analyzed. It is important to remember that the students who were in the remedial group are likely those who have continuously struggled in one or more academic subjects from year-to-year. Traditionally, these students would struggle throughout the entire year while receiving little to no targeted assistance. The reason that this is important to remember is that the growth these students show on the data sheets would normally never occur, as they would never have had the opportunty to receive targeted interventions at the very first sign of struggle.

It is also important to remember that not all students will respond to the provided remediation and teams need to identify patterns of student growth and lack of growth in order to identify the most effective intervention strategies for their students. Just as the original assessment data was examined, so too is the reassessment data. The team should be identifying patterns in growth or lack thereof, while identifying average student growth. This will inform the team of the effectiveness of the given intervention strategies.

After everyone has had an opportunity to review the reassessment, data teachers should begin to share the instructional strategies used during their intervention block. This conversation may look a little different depending on how the PLC had decided to divide up its students. If multiple teachers in the PLC had groups of students who were in the remediation cluster, then a comparison of student growth per teacher should be used to begin to identify the best remedial practices. However, if only one teacher on the team had the students in need of remedial assistance then that teacher should share out what they did and what they felt worked well and what could have worked better. The team should then come together and brainstorm possible ways to improve that remedial instruction and student performance. These instructional strategies should be added to lesson plans, as well as to the curriculum guide (See Figure 6.3).

Guiding the Conversation

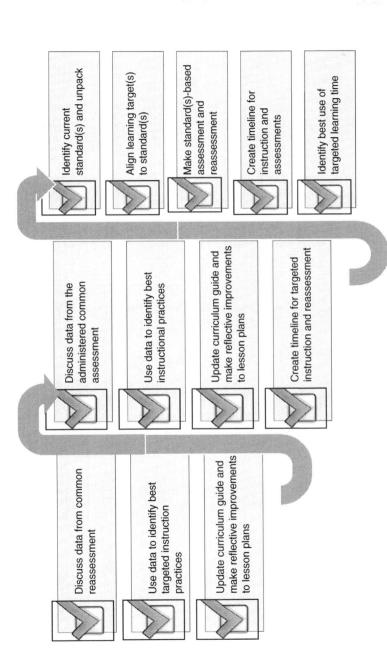

Figure 6.3 Third Meeting Agenda.

81

Guiding the Conversation

Meeting Overlaps

Depending on the pacing or assessment schedule, a PLC may commonly find its meetings have overlapping needs and agenda items that need to be discussed. For example, a team may have reassessment data to review, as well as first assessment data from a standard that was just finished, or they are reviewing unit assessment data and planning for the next instructional unit. There are multiple ways to approach this and in my experiences they are all equally effective and teams should simply do what works best for them.

The first option is to conduct all overlapping segments in the normally scheduled meeting time and pick up any "left over" pieces after school. This strategy usually works best for teams that are well organized and work together smoothly with each person pulling their weight equally and staying on task. Those groups that get straight to the point of each meeting will commonly find that a 40-minute block provides ample time to conduct all meeting business on the majority of occasions.

The second option is to intentionally split the meetings into separate segments. For example, a team may decide to have one meeting time that they use for planning a unit, making common assessments, and assigning appropriate learning targets. Then they may have another meeting whose sole purpose is data analysis. The only caveat with this approach is that teams will still need to complete all necessary items within the same timeframe. For example, if PLCs are meeting once a week to complete all tasks as described above then any team wanting to split up their meeting times will have to meet twice as often within the same time frame. So, if during the month of October, the 3rd-grade team meets four times and completes all agenda items in each meeting, the 4th grade team—that chooses to split up its meetings—would have to meet eight times.

Teams should have the freedom to choose whichever of these methods works best for them and have the ability to experiment with both in order to find the best fit, so long as they are able to work out the logistical aspect of each. Regardless of what option a team chooses, the process and outcome remains the same.

82

Conclusion

Having clear and attainable expectations is part of leadership; however, these expectations most also be understood by those who are supposed to be meeting them. Teachers should have an understanding of what will be happening and what they will need to bring to each meeting. They should also know the goals and purpose of each meeting. There should be a clear agenda that can be easily referenced for each meeting as well as established norms in order to ensure that the meetings stay on topic and progress smoothly.

As mentioned in Chapter 2, the logistical components of this process are ongoing and must be identified and planned in order to smoothly facilitate this process while ensuring that you get the most out of the scheduled time.

Avoiding Common Pitfalls

Introduction

The purpose of this chapter is to help districts, schools, and teams avoid common mistakes and unneeded stress in the PLC process. Both administrators and teachers have enough to worry about without adding unnecessary and avoidable conflict to the daily mix. Even if you follow all of the advice in this chapter there may still be a few unpredicted roadblocks to navigate, however they should be relatively isolated instances and will likely be logistical in nature.

Focus on Core Instruction

Although I spend a large amount of time in this book talking about planning for and targeting students with appropriate interventions, it must be duly noted that there is no substitute for good teaching. When done properly the PLC process focuses on the improvement of core instruction prior to everything else. In fact, the entire process of focusing on and aligning specific standards, as well as the initial common assessments, is a focus on identifying good core instruction. The modifications of lesson plans, integration of new instructional strategies, and more rigorous tasks are all meant to improve the core.

Avoiding Common Pitfalls

> Without a strong core, teams will not be able to provide truly targeted focus on those students who truly need it.

Without a strong core, teams will not be able to provide truly targeted focus on those students who truly need it. If the core instruction is weak, there will not be enough time or personnel to provide ample interventions. Any framework that promotes targeted and specific interventions, including PLCs and Response to Instruction (RTI), focuses first on strengthening the core instruction instead of being forced to provide remediation to everyone.

There should be noticeable improvements to core delivery throughout this process. It will likely be gradual, but it should be noticeable. Evidence of this should be clearly articulated in lesson plans, as they should be evolving to adopt best practices. Average proficiency scores should also begin to ascend on the common assessments as best practices are integrated. It is easy, and unfortunately quite common, for teams to unintentionally gloss over the role and actual affect of core instruction. In a real-life scenario provided by City et al. (2009), the team's data made it quite apparent that student learning was accruing at different rates from one class to the next. The team discussed perceived differences in each class that could explain the differing results and each teacher offered an explanation that rationalized the varying achievement levels of the classes. The team quickly resolved that the differences were attributed to each class's skill level at the beginning of the unit. As a result the conversation swiftly moved to what remedial strategies the team would implement.

City et al. (2009) point out that, through observing the classroom instruction, it was easily apparent that the actual work which was occurring in each of these classrooms was quite different, even though all teachers were working within a common curricular framework. The level of student achievement that each teacher reported at the PLC meeting directly correlated to the level of the tasks that each of these teachers were requiring of their students. You see, the differences in student performance were directly related to the teaching that was actually taking place and the tasks that the students were instructed to complete. As the authors so cleverly point out: "This was yet more evidence for a simple, but powerful lesson—hold on to your hats—*teaching causes learning*" (p. 28).

85

If all that the members of your team, school, or district focuses on is remediating students who do not meet the established proficiency mark, the growth you attain from the PLC process will quickly plateau. By moving the focus away from improving core instruction, via the dissection and explanation of instruction and student tasks, you are removing the "learning" from Professional Learning Community. It is the continuous improvement to core instruction that will continuously improve student achievement and build teacher capacity. PLCs simply provide a forum and process for this to take place.

A system of intervention, no matter how powerful or well organized, can never make up for bad teaching. Although remediating students for learning is a vital piece of the process, you cannot focus solely on these strategies and techniques. A school that focuses exclusively on student remediation will fail to build both teacher and administrator effectiveness and will ultimately fail to ever become a Professional Learning Community (DuFour et al., 2004).

Teams often want to jump directly into the remediation phase of the process without ever truly focusing on and discussing their delivery of the core instruction. This can sometimes be attributed to a simple misunderstanding of the purpose and power of a PLC. Or it may be that the process was presented only as a means or framework for remediation. However, there is quite frequently another, far more innocent, explanation for this.

Beware the Land of Nice

It has been ingrained in the culture of educators to be "nice" to each other and that giving any type of feedback or constructive criticism is a personal affront. This is largely because educators view their practice, style, and methodology as a part of who they are, and when others critique the way they teach, they are in fact critiquing and insulting the individual (City et al., 2009).

The misconception that one is defined by the way one teaches is a particularly absurd and illogical roadblock that continues to hamper teacher and student growth across the county. The belief that we as professionals cannot maturely and tactfully give and receive feedback is abhorrent to what we do every day as educators and what we expect our students to do everyday. We are *all* students, *all* the time, and just as we expect our students to learn and grow through the instruction and feedback we give them, so must we learn and grow—hence the name Professional Learning Community.

Some people can make collaboration seem more like a chore, and it is likely that these individuals have been poisoning the well for quite some time. Make no mistake, this process leaves these people no place to hide and will likely bring their unprofessional behaviors to center stage. The PLC process requires and promotes professional growth through collaboration and change.

City et al. (2009) describe professionals as people who share a common practice, not those whose taste and style determines their practice. They go on to reflect that viewing one's practice as a matter of individual taste is largely anti-professional. Professionals act upon and integrate the best and most efficient strategies and continue to modify their techniques and practices with new data-based evidence.

If one is unwilling to operate based on reflective practice and data-driven results, one should not receive the distinction of being considered a professional. Just imagine if other practitioners or companies operated under the same mind-set that some educators do and never changed their business practices or adapted their products based on customer feedback, sales, or critiques from the market? The conclusive fact is that any company operating like this wouldn't be in business for long, and educators operating like this shouldn't be allowed to stay in business either.

What if medical practitioners failed to examine the results of their work and failed to follow up with patients after an operation? This would be much like the traditional testing procedures many educators still use. Or, what if a doctor followed up with a patient and failed to respond to the data. Imagine the reaction you would have if, after an operation, your doctor came in and said: "Well, it looks like your incision is infected…that's really too bad… alright, well I have to go, maybe a doctor can fix it for you next year…good luck with everything." This is just like educators looking at student data, but not doing anything with it. Educators operate on the minds of students every single day, how can we not be reflective of and responsive to the work we do?

Collaboration

The process of collaboration can symbolize different actions for different people and is often times confused with congeniality or a misrepresented

Avoiding Common Pitfalls

form of collegiality. Within the various teams in a school you will see those who exhibit strong congeniality, meaning they like each other and get along well, and collegiality, meaning they divide the workload. As a school leader you may mistake the above groups for a team that is truly collaborative in nature. Of course we want all of our teams to be collegial and congenial, but it isn't until true collaboration takes place that student achievement will increase. Many times teachers will think they are a collaborative team, when in fact they just divide up the workload. Addressing misconceptions of what true collaboration is and what it looks like is critical to the success of the PLC process. It is important to understand how true collaboration benefits the PLC and what to look for when team members are interacting to insure that the process is beneficial.

Supervisors appreciate it when team members interact positively with one another and benefit from congenial relationships. However, groups with cozy relationships do not automatically translate into high-functioning collaborative teams. At times these groups may struggle with confronting their data or giving each other honest feedback out of fear of jeopardizing their congenial team dynamic. It is through the existence of professional trust and respect that team members will develop the interpersonal security needed to have truly open conversation with their peers. Members of great teams trust one another and are comfortable being vulnerable with each other about their weaknesses and their mistakes. Teams that trust one another are not afraid to engage in critical conversations around issues and decisions that are crucial for student success. Teams who trust one another do not hesitate to disagree, challenge, and question each other. They hold each other accountable and will likely set aside their own needs to focus on what is best for students.

The preexistence of congenial team dynamics can serve as a great springboard for success, but if the congeniality is masking the insecurity of having the data-driven conversations that are necessary to stimulate true reflective practice, it needs to be promptly addressed. This can be done strategically through team building activities and carefully guided conversation.

When collegiality is misrepresented in the PLC process, teams will appear to make progress toward their common goals, but the actual purpose for having PLCs will be lost. Consider this example.

> A PLC may believe that they exemplify collaboration because they have equally divided the workload. Teacher A writes the

Avoiding Common Pitfalls

lesson plans, Teacher B makes the assessments, and Teacher C uploads the data and divides students into their targeted instruction groups. The team members meet in their PLC, distribute their work, site a few key points, and move on.

In a case such as this it can easily appear that the team is high functioning and effective. Everyone has a defined role and on the surface it can appear that everyone is working together. However, what is actually occurring is that everyone is working in isolation in order to lessen the workload. This practice, in and of it self, is not necessarily a bad thing, but it does nothing to build teacher capacity and likely only reduces their capacity as they have no involvement in the process outside of their isolated task. As teams become more collaborative in nature, school leaders will see a shared responsibility for the success of all students, and mutual accountability and responsibility among faculty and administrative staff.

Both Chapter 4 and Chapter 6 acknowledge that our time is finite, and that it is permissible, and at times recommended, to split the workload. Many tasks leave little choice other than to share or divide the responsibilities in order to complete a given task. However, this must be done with the understanding that the team will make the time to collaboratively review each task that was completed in isolation. This will ensure that both the finished product and the team members are enriched by the collaborative effort.

Getting Started

As stated in the previous chapters, so much of the success and ease of integration of this process hinges on taking the time to thoroughly and properly plan. There is a colorful saying that basically states "poor planning creates poor results." This could not be better exemplified than in this process. Not only do administrators and teams need to take the time to think and plan this process all the way through, but they also need to include other stakeholders in the planning process.

This process involves the classroom teachers on every level and through every step, so it only makes sense that they are part of the planning process. Having a small team of teachers give feedback during the planning process may require a little bit of time on the front end, but will pay

89

huge dividends on the flip side, while also saving an administrator valuable time and stress fighting unnecessary battles. I have always found that creating forums to receive teacher feedback has only made the process more effective than it ever could have been if I simply did everything on my own. Your teachers should be the experts in their field and should be more in tune with their needs, difficulties, and potential scheduling conflicts than any single supervisor could hope to be.

Depending on what the needs of your school are, there may be a lot of prior planning that must be done to facilitate this process, and depending on when you plan on implementing this process you may need to get things done sooner rather than later. If you are on a tight deadline, having a single committee or team assist with the planning of all the pieces of this entire process may not be the most effective use of your time. So long as everyone has been given a clear expectation of the ending goals and finish line, you could implement a "work-in-progress protocol" (Jackson, 2013). Jackson refers to this as a method of selecting a few teachers for multiple teams, each of which could work on a specific item then bring that item back to the larger group and present what they have been working on. The group then has an opportunity to provide feedback and questions to the presenters, who have an opportunity to respond to their feedback and seek any clarification of the feedback. The presenters would then go back and attempt to further refine their approach before bringing it back to the group. Theoretically, this could speed up the planning process by two or three times.

Too Much Too Soon

I get it. You want growth and you want it now. You've done all the logistical prep work with your master schedule, you've organized appropriate support for both teachers and students during the targeted learning block, you've set up common planning times among grade levels and content areas. You have done all the proper training and involved all the necessary stakeholders. Everyone is anxious, excited, on-board, ready to go, head first, all in, let's do this!

Ready…set—STOP!

In my experiences, one of the biggest and most common mistakes that schools make is that they take on too much too soon. When first starting

Avoiding Common Pitfalls

this process you must identify what subjects (elementary) or what sections (secondary) you are going to start with. Without grasping the true volume of work this process takes (especially when first starting), educators can quickly become overwhelmed and tempted to prematurely throw in the towel. This experience may also pave the way down to the all-too-common scenario of "let's meet just to say we did." This happens because there is realistically no way to do everything all at once while keeping one's sanity.

It is not only unrealistic, but also completely unfair, to task schools and teachers with a mandate to tackle all of their content areas and preps with this process when starting from zero. The same philosophy that applies to encouraging teachers to teach for learning and not just coverage of the content applies to the implementation of this process.

For elementary schools, or those whose teachers keep the same group of children for the majority of the day and teach all the core subjects, you must select a subject to start with that will remain the focus for the first year. Do not start with both Language Arts and Math. Choose one, and only one.

It will be the goal of each grade level to thoroughly complete all aspects of this process in one of these chosen subjects. This will allow teams to provide ample focus and attention to improve this one area before adding another. I recommend that the entire school choose the same subject and that the subject is chosen using both logic and data. This will allow your teams to share some resources and strategies that may work across grade levels, while also making it easier to monitor growth. If your school has an obvious deficiency in one subject then that should be the selected subject.

However, if there is not an obvious school-wide deficiency in one subject I would recommend starting with Language Arts. The rational for this is multifaceted. First, if students can't comprehend grade-level reading material then they will struggle in all other subjects. Second, reading assessments are almost always more difficult to compose and their resources are scarcer, thus requiring a higher investment of time on the part of the teachers. It is generally better to take on the more difficult of the subjects in the first year, when it is the only area of focus. The first year is the only time when the teams will have just one area to focus all of their attention, so make it count.

For secondary schools, or those that organize their teachers by content area, you must select a starting point from which to build. For this example, I will use the English department and will assume that the school offers English I, II, III, and IV. The team will need to sort out all the teachers who teach English I, those who teach English II but not English I, those who teach English III but not I or II, and those who teach only English IV. The rationale for this deals mostly with personnel and time constraints.

Everyone who teaches English I needs to be part of that PLC and needs to be fully involved in the common assessment, targeted instruction, and reassessment processes. Just as the teams in the elementary school need the ability to completely focus on one subject area, so must secondary teachers be afforded the same opportunity to put their best foot forward and focus on making something great and powerful, instead of being spread too thin and losing their effectiveness.

If everyone in the department teaches a section of English I, then that will be the sole focus of that department for the first year. Then the school or department can add English II the following year, and then III and IV during the third and fourth years of implementation.

However, if the department has pockets of teachers who are isolated and don't teach all sections, then the department may be able to begin this process in two or more sections of the same subject area, so long as no teacher is being left out of a PLC for a section that they teach, and no teacher is required to attend a PLC for more then one section in the first year.

There is one partial exception to this that I have seen implemented with great success—although limited to those teams that have excellent working relationships and strong teacher leadership. Motivated teams that are able to quickly adapt to this process may want to get a head start on what they know is coming the following year, and may feel confident in their ability to take more on their proverbial plate. Although it would be rarely advised for these teams to jump full bore into another subject or section, they may choose to begin making and implementing the first round of common of assessments (no reassessments should take place at this time) for each of their standards, goals, or skills for whichever subject or section is going to be added the following year. Teams should never be forced to do this and should never take on this additional task prior to showing an aptitude for the first subject or section of focus.

Presence

Administrator presence and leadership is essential in this process. The first and most obvious reason for this is that one has to be willing to check what one expects. If an administrator brings a new process and framework for

Avoiding Common Pitfalls

improving student learning and teacher effectiveness, but is unwilling to be actively involved in that process, then it is sure to fail. No matter how well intentioned an administrator is, if they are not willing to actively monitor and support an initiative—no matter how small or large in scope—by the time they figure out things aren't going the way they should be the year will likely be wasted and the student growth that could have taken place will, yet again, take a back seat.

In the PLC process the majority of the monitoring and support for the process happens during the actual PLC meetings. This should come as no surprise since this is where the majority of the data analysis and instructional dialog will take place.

If, as an administrator, you are still not convinced that you need to be an active participant in your school's PLCs, then I would ask you to consider this: Your job, as a school-based administrator, is to provide supervision and leadership to your school and staff. This is something I believe we can all agree to be a simple and inarguable truth. Even though the exact details of the job usually require random day-to-day nuances, you were hired, primarily, to provide supervision and leadership, in all of its various forms and capacities. So to frame it in a logical and irrefutable manner—it is *your* job to help supervise and lead your staff. Period.

> It is not best practice for a teacher to deliver their instruction from behind a desk, it is not best practice for an administrator to provide leadership from behind an office door.

This process cannot be properly done if the school-based administrator is not part of the process. The same way we know that it is not best practice for a teacher to deliver their instruction from behind a desk, it is not best practice for an administrator to provide leadership from behind an office door.

Functionality

Not every PLC will look and sound the same, and that's okay. Some will use different intervention and remediation strategies and methods, some will have a clear leader driving the conversation, and others will be more fluid and the internal leadership may seem more autonomous. These differences are of little concern so long as the established framework and objectives are being followed. A high-functicning team should be identified through its contributions to student learning and growth and their adherence to the given objectives and framework. Frameworks and objectives may vary school-to-school or district-to-district depending on preexisting resources such as pacing guides, schedules, and academic calendars.

Educators should be aware that not every team or grade level in a school shares the same dynamic or working relationship. In fact, many teams suffer from strained relationships and for some of these teams their relationships may hamper the ability or willingness of the team to work together. For these—hopefully uncommon—scenarios I offer some simple advice: "start by getting the right people on the bus, the wrong people off the bus, and the right people in the right seats" (Collins, 2001). Children should never suffer simply because adults can't get it together.

I find that, within most dysfunctional groups, it is usually the case of one bad apple or one poor relationship that ruins what would otherwise be an excellent team dynamic. Where a team is unable to come to terms with internal relationship issues on its own, it is the responsibility of the site-based administrator to make the necessary modifications to the team or grade-level composition. It may be necessary to move an individual to a different grade level or different course sections. However, if one person's personality is simply too toxic, and that individual can't find the internal control to do what's best for the kids, then proper documentation can usually see that toxicity removed from the building for the benefit of all parties. I don't promote the idea that administrators go looking for confrontation just to satisfy an ego or power trip. It is, however, an expectation that administrators have the courage and confidence to address and properly handle personnel issues in their building, especially when these issues jeopardize the ability of the school to provide the best possible education for and opportunities to its students.

Just as site-based administrators are responsible for ensuring that those at their building are following the appropriate protocol, district-level administrators are responsible for ensuring that those at the school level are appropriately monitoring and leading their schools.

"All or Nothing" Versus "Something Is Better than Nothing"

When examining the PLC process it may be easy to become intimidated by the amount of prep work involved in setting up the foundation to support it and all its protocols. There may be too little time prior to the start of the coming year to make any meaningful and well-thought-out changes that won't haphazardly cause more problems than they will solve. Or maybe it is the middle of the year and simply not feasible to change the master schedule without promoting complete and total chaos. So you're left with the option of doing nothing until you are "ready," next year (maybe), or doing something, but not everything—wait and do a full-fledged rollout, or start with a piecemeal approach?

This can be a tough call, and may be situational in nature. If you are more than halfway through a school year, or semester, it will likely make most sense to hold off and ensure you have the time to both put a solid plan in place and properly educate and involve your staff in the process.

However, if your school or team already has many of the foundational pieces in place, such as common planning times, pacing guides, and consistent collaboration on lessons and activities, then you may be ready to move forward in some areas, regardless of what time of the year it is. In situations such as this there is no reason teachers can't start working on and implementing common assessments, although I would recommend abstaining from the remediation protocols until all logistical issues have been considered.

No matter how ill prepared you may feel to properly implement the PLC process, at some point you have to make the decision to cast off the excuses and start. It doesn't matter how much literature you read or how many people you consult, the only way to actually learn and improve upon the process is to actually start the process. If you never start, you will never reap any of the gains.

Planning, discussing, holding committee and school-improvement meetings will only get you so far. If you never actually "do anything" you will never actually get, learn, grow, or improve anything. Therefore, in the vast majority of cases I would strongly suggest that something *is* better than nothing. Even if you don't feel comfortable tackling the entire process at once, I implore you to at least do something, and then build on the process each year. Just be sure to set logical and time-bound goals for implementing the entire process. A staggered rollout for this process should mirror something similar to the following:

Year 1: Focus on the Core:

- Set up pacing guides and protocols for unpacking standards.
- Establish common planning times per grade levels or contents.
- Schedule weekly PLC meetings in order to:
    - Format and integrate common assessments (per standard and unit).
    - Discuss best practices and integrate into lesson plans (ongoing).
- Start and maintain proper curriculum guides (ongoing).

Year 2: Focus on Individual Student Learning Needs:

- Continue refining all Year 1 protocols.
- Establish targeted learning block to immediately respond to student needs for a single subject or content of focus.
- Implement common reassessments in order to measure student learning after interventions in order to:
    - Analyze intervention data (ongoing).
    - Adopt and adapt best practice (ongoing).
- Continue to update and maintain curriculum guides (ongoing).

Year 3: Expand and Refine:

- Continue refining all Year 1 and Year 2 protocols.
- Expand targeted learning block(s) and common reassessments to accommodate additional subject(s) and contents(s) in order to:
    - Analyze intervention data (ongoing).
    - Adopt and adapt best practice (ongoing).
- Continue to update and maintain curriculum guides (ongoing).

Year 4: Refining:

- Continue refining all protocols of the process.

Conclusion

> By properly planning for and being aware of potential concerns, you can ensure that no obstacle will be dramatic enough to derail you on your road to success.

I have listed and explained some of the common pitfalls that can occur when beginning and implementing PLCs. However, it is quite possible that you will experience obstacles that I have not identified. Remember that, no matter what obstacles you encounter, every problem has a solution and every question has an answer. By properly planning for and being aware of potential concerns, you can ensure that no obstacle will be dramatic enough to derail you on your road to success.

References

City, E., Elmore, R., Fiarman, S., & Teitel, L. (2009). *Instructional Rounds in Education: A Network Approach to Improving Teaching and Learning.* Cambridge, MA: Harvard Education Press.

Collins, J. (2001). *Good to Great.* Retrieved on 3 October, 2015 from http://www.jimcollins.com/article_topics/articles/good-to-great.html

DuFour, R., DuFour, R., Eaker, R., & Karhanek, G. (2004). *Whatever It Takes: How Professional Learning Communities Respond When Kids Don't Learn.* Bloomington, IN: Solution Tree Press.

Jackson, R. (2013). *Never Underestimate Your Teachers: Instructional Leadership for Excellence in Every Classroom.* Alexandria, VA: ASCD.

Putting It All Together

I believe that your time is too valuable to waste, and that if you are going to invest your time on something that is supposed to help your students to be more successful and better prepared for the future, then it better work. I don't want you to gamble a child's future on something that *might* yield results. I want you to secure the future of more children by doing something that *will* work. You must demand a guarantee that whatever initiative you're going to implement is going to help yield tangible results and visible growth.

Mapping out the Process, Foundations, and Protocols

Properly implementing PLCs in your district or school is not a gamble; it is an irrefutable promise of growth. It's like knowing the next winning lottery numbers, except you don't have to be clairvoyant or have had a conversation with your future self in order to win. Just follow the steps, understand the process, build your foundation, and plan your protocols.

Understanding what the process is supposed to look like is an essential first step. If you don't understand how each part of the process fits together then you will never benefit fully from it, and you will find great difficulty in building both a foundation and protocols to support the process. Each and every item indicated below is an essential part of this process. Comprehending and appreciating each of these steps will alleviate many of the headaches and inefficiencies that some people encounter when they haven't taken the time to map out and plan their success.

Understanding the Process

1. Meet with your PLC
   - Identify current standard(s) and unpack
   - Align learning target(s) to standard(s)
   - Make standard(s)-based assessment *and* reassessment
   - Create timeline for instruction and assessments
2. Introduce learning target to students
   - Utilize day-to-day assessments to guide instruction
   - Use targeted learning time to do preventative maintenance and enrichment
3. Administer standard(s)-based common assessment
4. Meet with your PLC
   - Discuss data from common assessment
   - Identify best instructional practices
   - Update curriculum guide and make reflective improvements to lesson plans
   - Plan interventions based on data
   - Establish timeline for remediation, interventions, maintenance, and enrichment
5. Conduct remediation, interventions, maintenance, and enrichment
6. Reassess students who did not initially meet proficiency and received remedial instruction
   - Discuss results, monitor growth, record what worked and what did not
7. Repeat

After you have familiarized yourself with the PLC process you must examine your foundation. Undoubtedly, there are some pieces that are already in place and may need only minor tweaking. Other areas may be completely absent and must be planned and set in place prior to implementing the corresponding part of the process. It is in the foundational planning that you should decide if you will do a staggered rollout of the PLC process, or if you are ready to go all in and achieve maximum growth.

Putting It All Together

Examine Your Foundation

1. Review or begin creation of pacing guides
   - Do you have logical, current and up-to-date pacing guides?
   - Do your pacing guides give attention to priority standards?
   - Do you have a process for unpacking standards or is it assumed that everyone is already intimately familiar with them?
2. Identify current status and current framework of existing PLCs
   - What's working, what's not, and how do you know?
   - Is your current structure examining relevant data?
   - Is that data being acted upon?
3. Establish common planning times
   - Do daily common planning times exist within each grade level or content area?
   - Are teams using this time to work and plan together?
4. Time for targeted interventions
   - Has your master schedule already been adapted to fit a targeted learning block?
   - If yes—What's working, and what's not?
   - Are support staff and specialists scheduled to maximize the effectiveness of this block?
   - If no—Do you have time to reorganize the schedule before the next school year?
   - Are there scheduling committees that could assist? Would they understand the purpose?
5. Capacity
   - Identify current team, staff, and/or district understanding of the PLC process across the district
   - How will current deficiencies or misunderstandings be addressed prior to or during the rollout?
   - How will school-based leaders make their staff a part of this process in order to generate buy-in, understanding, and ownership while also ensuring that the process continues regardless of school leadership?

After identifying existing foundational pieces and recognizing which others need to be added or improved, protocols must be applied to each. A protocol informs someone exactly how something is supposed to be done. It ensures that, as long as steps A to Z are followed, the desired results should be achieved. There is no reason that protocols can't be added, taken away, or changed to better fit a particular need. However, the changing of protocols should not be ad hoc. There should literally be protocols for adding, taking away, or changing protocols. This will ensure that all involved parties are properly informed of potential changes and some aren't left doing the same thing less efficiently than others. Although it is impossible to plan for every eventuality, planning protocols for the questions and statements below will start you on the path to growth.

Plan Your Protocols

1. How will pacing guides be reviewed?
2. What is the process for unpacking standards?
3. What days and times will PLCs meet?
4. Establish norms and expectations for each PLC meeting.
5. Is there a selected format the student-generated data should be placed in, who will do it, and when?
6. How will curriculum guides be built and maintained?
7. How will each team or school appropriately identify and target learning needs during the intervention block?
   - How and when will the success or failure of these interventions be determined, discussed, recorded, and improved upon?
8. How will protocols and processes be planned, modified, or added?

Understanding the PLC framework in its entirety is the first step. It is the overview of what needs to be done and informs you of what the destination is. The problem with understanding only the framework is that, even though it gives you the destination, it doesn't tell you how to get there. It tells what has to be done, but not how to do it. It is like having a map that only shows your current location and destination, but leaves out all of the streets and highways in between. Adding and understanding the processes is like knowing the streets you're supposed to turn at, but not knowing which way to turn. The protocols are the details that guide you through the

Putting It All Together

step-by-step directions that see you safely to your destination. The success of the PLC process, like most others, lies with recognizing your foundational needs and planning your protocols.

Commitment

Once you have made the decision to implement PLCs you must also make a commitment to see the process through. It doesn't make any sense for educators to continue working in silos where the quality of students' education is dependent on what teacher they are lucky or unlucky enough to get. We must make a commitment to team-based learning communities through PLCs in order to build an internal capacity that will guarantee student learning and growth regardless of school or district resources. Effective team-based learning is the best kind of professional development by encouraging teachers to recognize, share, and improve upon the very best of what they already know (Schmoker, 2006).

> Just stating that you are doing PLCs doesn't get results. You have to be committed to doing the process correctly, not just in name.

Just stating that your doing PLCs doesn't get results. You have to be committed to doing the process correctly, not just in name. Vince Lombardi, a well-known expert on winning, states that, "You don't do things right once in a while…you do them right all the time" (Lombardi and Lombardi, 2006, p. 7). So if you're going to do PLCs it's only rational that you do them fully and that you do them correctly. You have to make doing the right thing so habitual that not doing it appears offensive or criminal in nature. Refuse to accept excuses from either yourself, or your team, and show that you have the discipline to see your commitment through. Remember, this isn't about you and me: it's about doing what's best for our kids.

You can have the continual growth and success you say you want, or you can have all the excuses about why your school can't attain them, but you can't have both. You have to make the choice: do you want excuses or do you want results? Do you want to lead positive change, or do you want to follow the ways things have always been done?

The time for action is now, and the choice is yours.

So, what are you waiting for?

References

Lombardi, V., & Lombardi, V., Jr. (2006). *What It Takes to Be Number One*. Naperville, IL: SimpleTruths.

Schmoker, M. (2006). *Results Now*. Alexandria, VA: ASCD.

Appendix

Enter Subject and Level (Target Score 77/100)
Enter Standard(s) or Skill(s) and/or Title

Student	Class 1	Retest		Class 2	Retest		Class 3	Retest
1								
2								
3								
4								
5								
6								
7								
8								
9								
10								
11								
12								
13								
14								
15								
16								
17								
18								
19								
20								
21								
22								
23								
Avg. Score								

Figure A1   Sample Data Form 1.

Appendix

Enter Subject and Level (Target Score) Standards/Skills

Student Number	Assessment 1 Author's Purpose	Assessment 2 Reassessment	Growth	Assessment 1 Cause and Effect	Assessment 2 Reassessment	Growth	Assessment 1 Theme	Assessment 2 Reassessment	Growth	Assessment 1 Unit Test
1										
2										
3										
4										
5										
6										
7										
8										
9										
10										
11										
12										
13										
14										
15										
16										
17										
18										
19										
20										
21										
22										
23										
Totals										

Figure A2 Sample Data Form 2.

SAMPLE - Elementary Master Schedule

Grade K	Unpack MW	Literacy	Targeted Ins. Literacy	Math	Lunch	Targeted Ins. Math	Recess	SCI/SS	Centers	Read Aloud
	8:00-8:20	8:20-9:30	9:30-10:00	10:00-11:00	11:00-11:30	12:00-12:30	12:30-1:00	1:00-1:30	1:30-2:15	2:15-2:25

Grade 1	Math	Targeted Ins. Math	Literacy	Targeted Ins. Literacy	Lunch	Sustained Silent Reading	Recess	SCI	SS	Read Aloud
	8:15-9:00	9:00-9:30	9:30-10:15	10:15-11:00	11:15-11:45	12:00-12:30	12:30-1:00	1:00-1:40	1:40-2:15	2:15-2:25

Grade 2	Targeted Ins. Literacy	Literacy	Math	Recess	Targeted Ins. Math	Lunch	Sustained Silent Reading	SCI	SS	Read Aloud
	8:15-9:00	9:00-9:45	9:45-10:30	10:30-11:00	11:00-11:30	11:30-12:00	12:15-1:00	1:00-1:40	1:40-2:15	2:15-2:25

Grade 3	Math	Literacy	Recess	SCI/SS	Lunch	Sustained Silent Reading	Targeted Ins. Math	Targeted Ins. Literacy	Read Aloud
	8:15-9:30	9:30-10:30	10:30-11:00	11:00-11:30	11:45-12:15	12:30-1:00	1:00-1:30	1:30-2:15	2:15-2:25

Grade 4	Math	Sci/SS	Reading	Targeted Ins. Literacy	Lunch	Targeted Ins. Math	Recess	Read Aloud/ Sustained Silent Reading
	8:15-9:15	9:15-10:15	10:15-11:15	11:15-12:00	12:05-12:35	12:45-1:30	1:30-2:00	2:00-2:25

Grade 5	Math	Targeted Ins. Math	Literacy	Science	Recess	Lunch	Sustained Silent Reading	Targeted Ins. Literacy	Read Aloud
	8:15-9:15	9:15-9:45	9:45-10:45	10:45-11:30	11:30-12:00	12:20-12:50	1:00-1:30	1:30-2:15	2:15-2:25

Figure A3   Sample Elementary Master Schedule – Submitted by Denton Elementary, Davidson County.

Appendix

EC Specialist: Teacher Name

Time	Grade	Subject
8:15-9:00	2	Literacy
9:00-9:30	1	Math
9:30-10:00	K	Literacy
10:15-11:00	1	Literacy
11:00-11:30	2	Math
11:30-12:00	Lunch	
12:00-12:30	K	Math
12:30-1:00	Plan	
1:00-1:30	3	Math
1:30-2:15	3	Literacy

EC Specialist: Teacher Name

Time	Grade	Subject
8:15-8:45	5	Math/Inclusion
8:45-9:15	4	Math/Inclusion
9:15-9:45	5	Math IME
9:45-10:15	5	Lit./Inclusion
10:15-10:45	4	Lit./Inclusion
10:45-11:15	Plan	
11:15-12:00	4	Literacy/IME
12:00-12:30	Lunch	
12:45-1:30	4	Math IME
1:30-2:15	5	Literacy IME

Literacy Specialist: Teacher Name

Time	Grade	
8:15-9:00	2	Targeted Ins.
9:00-9:30	Plan	
9:30-10:00	K	Targeted Ins.
10:15-11:00	1	Targeted Ins.
11:00-11:30	Plan	
11:30-12:00	Lunch	
12:00-12:30	1	Targeted Ins.
12:30-1:00	2	Targeted Ins.
1:30-2:15	3	Targeted Ins.

Math Specialist: Teacher Name

Time	Grade	
9:00-9:30	1	Targeted Ins.
9:45-10:30	2	Push In
10:30-11:00	K	Push In
11:00-11:30	2	Targeted Ins.
11:30-12:00	Plan	
12:00-12:30	K	Targeted Ins.
12:30-1:00	Lunch	
1:00-1:30	3	Targeted Ins.
1:30-2:00	Plan	

Figure A3 (Continued).

In developing the master schedule, we wanted to find a way for all students to remain in class to receive core instruction. We also wanted to provide enough staff during targeted instruction time to allow groups to remain small to remediate students' most foundational skill deficiencies. Scheduling in this manner afforded the school both of these important components. This approach assisted the school in growing students across grade levels as demonstrated in increased proficiencies on end of grade tests.

Kathern Green – Principal, Denton Elementry

Appendix

	Grade 5	Grade 4	Grade 3	Grade 2	Grade 1	Kindergarten
7:50	Unpack	Unpack	Unpack	Unpack	Unpack	Unpack
8:00	Targeted Instruction	Reading	Reading	Writing	Phonics	Phonics
8:10						
8:20						
8:30	Science			Science	Reading	Reading
8:40						
8:50						
9:00						
9:10		Targeted Instruction		Math		
9:20						
9:30	Social Studies/ Writing					
9:40		Reading	Targeted Instruction			
9:50						Math
10:00						
10:10					Science	
10:20	Reading	Science	Math	Social Studies		
10:30						
10:40						
10:50					Targeted Instruction	Writing
11:00				Lunch		
11:10						
11:20		Math	Social Studies	Targeted Instruction	Lunch	Read Aloud
11:30						
11:40						
11:50	Recess					Lunch
12:00			Lunch		Recess	
12:10				Reading		
12:20	Lunch	Lunch			Math	Targeted Instruction
12:30			Recess			
12:40						
12:50	Math	Social Studies	Read Aloud	Recess		Social Studies
1:00						
1:10						
1:20		Writing	Writing	Reading	Social Studies	Recess
1:30						
1:40						
1:50			Science			Pack Up/ Dismiss
2:00		Recess				
2:10						
2:20						

Figure A4 Sample Elementary Master Schedule – Submitted by Midway Elementary, Davidson County.

109

Appendix

Our master schedule reflects a staggered targeted intervention time for each grade level. Being a Non-Title 1 school and having no extra support specialist, we utilize all instructional assistants to support instruction during the targeted intervention block. The instructional assistant is utilized to work with students who have mastered the standard, based on common assessment data. The assistant provides high quality enrichment opportunities for those students while the teacher works with students needing remediation on the particular standard. The targeted intervention block is also utilized for students with special needs to be pulled by the exceptional children's teacher. By utilizing this block of time it ensures that our exceptional students are not missing core instruction while also providing time for the EC teacher to pull the student to work on missing foundational skills. The days that students have special classes (art, music, PE), the writing and Social Studies block is combined to provide time for special classes.

April Willard – Principal, Midway Elementary

Appendix

2015-2016 SDMS Daily Schedule

6th Grade		
Homeroom	7:55-8:38	Targeted Instruction
1st Period	8:40-9:44 (64)	Core
2nd Period	9:46-10:50 (64)	Core
3rd Period	10:52-11:56 (64)	Core
4th Period	11:58-1:28 (65+25)	Core/Lunch
5th Period	1:30-2:14 (44)	Encore/Planning
6th Period	2:16-3:00 (44)	Encore/Planning

7th Grade		
Homeroom	7:55-8:38	Targeted Instruction
1st Period	8:40-9:24 (44)	Encore/Planning
2nd Period	9:26-10:10 (44)	Encore/Planning
3rd Period	10:12-11:16 (64)	Core
4th Period	11:18-12:48 (65+25)	Core/Lunch
5th Period	12:50-1:54 (64)	Core
6th Period	1:56-3:00 (64)	Core

8th Grade		
Homeroom	7:55-8:38	Targeted Instruction
1st Period	8:40-9:44 (64)	Core
2nd Period	9:46-10:50 (64)	Core
3rd Period	10:52-11:36 (44)	Encore/Planning
4th Period	11:38-12:22 (44)	Encore/Planning
5th Period	12:24-1:54 (65+25)	Core/Lunch
6th Period	1:56-3:00 (64)	Core

Encore		
Homeroom	7:55-8:38	Targeted Instruction
1st Period	8:40-9:24 (44)	7th Grade
2nd Period	9:26 10:10 (44)	7th Grade
Planning	10:10 10:52 (42)	Planning
3rd Period	10:52-11:36 (44)	8th Grade
4th Period	11:38-12:22 (44)	8th Grade
Planning	12:22-1:30 (68)	Planning/Lunch
5th Period	1:30-2:14 (44)	6th Grade
6th Period	2:16-3:00 (44)	6th Grade

Figure A5 Sample Middle School Master Schedule – Submitted by South Davidson Middle School, Davidson County.

Appendix

8th Grade Targeted Instruction Groups

	Monday	Tuesday	Wednesday	Thursday
Group 1: Accelerated Math & High Reading (8)	Math Teacher (Enrichment)	Adaptive Online Software - Reading	Adaptive Online Software - Math	Reading Teacher (Enrichment)
Group 2: Accelerated Math & Struggling Reading (12)	Reading Teacher (Intervention)	Adaptive Online Software - Reading	Math Teacher (Enrichment)	Adaptive Online Software - Math
Group 3: High Reading & High Math (9)	Adaptive Online Software - Math	Reading Teacher (Enrichment)	Adaptive Online Software - Reading	Math Teacher (Enrichment)
Group 4: Proficient Reading & Proficient Math (11)	Adaptive Online Software - Reading	Reading Teacher (Maintenance)	Adaptive Online Software - Math	Math Teacher (Maintenance)
Group 5: Struggling Reading & Proficient Math (10)	Reading Teacher (Intervention)	Adaptive Online Software - Reading	Math Teacher (Maintenance)	Adaptive Online Software - Math
Group 6: Proficient Reading & Struggling Math (11)	Adaptive Online Software - Math	Math Teacher (Intervention)	Reading Teacher (Maintenance)	Adaptive Online Software - Reading
Group 7: Struggling Reading & Struggling Math (11)	Math Teacher (Intervention)	Adaptive Online Software - Math	Reading Teacher (Intervention)	Adaptive Online Software - Reading
Group 8: Low Reading & Low Math (10)	Adaptive Online Software - Reading	Math Teacher Remediation	Adaptive Online Software - Math	Reading Teacher Remediation
Group 9: Low Reading & Low Math (9)	Adaptive Online Software - Math	EC Teacher Remediation	Adaptive Online Software - Reading	EC Teacher Remediation
Group 10: Low Reading & Low Math (8)	EC Teacher Remediation	Adaptive Online Software - Math	EC Teacher Remediation	Adaptive Online Software - Reading

Figure A6 8th Grade targeted instruction groups.

South Davidson Middle School has taken a very strategic approach to incorporating targeted instruction into its academic day. Utilizing a staggered bell schedule, teachers are able to maximize their planning time. This additional time allows teachers to analyze create common assessments, analyze data, and structure groups for targeted instruction.

Targeted instruction groups, which occurs first thing in the morning, last approximately two weeks. Students are grouped with other students of similar ability level and receive teacher instruction aligned to their needs. Support staff monitor computer labs where adaptive online software is used to provide personalized instruction to all students. To ensure quick transitions students record their schedule in their student handbook. Schedules including only student names are also placed outside of every targeted instruction location. This intentional approach to making every minute count at SDMS is raising achievement and positively impacting student success.

Crystal Sexton - Principal, South Davidson Middle School

Appendix

E Lawson Brown Middle School - Master Schedule

6th Grade		7th Grade		8th Grade	
7:55-8:05	Homeroom	7:55-8:05	Homeroom	7:55-8:05	Homeroom
1st period	Intervention	1st period	Intervention	1st period	Intervention
2nd period	Core	2nd period	Core	2nd period	PE/Encore
3rd period	Core	3rd period	Core	3rd period	PE/Encore
4th period	Core/Lunch	4th period	PE/Encore	4th period	Core
5th period	Core	5th period	PE/Encore	5th period	Core/Lunch
6th period	PE/Encore	6th period	Core/Lunch	6th period	Core
7th period	PE/Encore	7th period	Core	7th period	Core

Four-week reading remediation and intervention block - Sample

EC	EC	Reading	SS Teacher	Science Teacher	Reading/ Social Studies	Math Teacher	Math Teacher/ SCI	Science/ Social Studies	Math/ Social Studies	Reading Specialist
EC	EC	Comprehension - Students 3 years below grade level	Comprehension - Students 2 years below grade level	Comprehension - Students 2 years below grade level	Comprehension - Students 1 year below grade level	Comprehension - Students 1 year below grade level	Comprehension - Students on grade level	Vocabulary	Phonics/ Voc.	Phonics/ HFW

Four-week problem/project-based learning groups for enrichment - Sample

PE	PE	PE	CTE	CTE	CTE	Band	Art	Music	Media
The Bat Cave	The World Around Us	Mats for the Homeless	Race to the Sun	Sports Center Live	When I Grow Up	That's Debateable	Bad Boys of History	Trash to Treasure	Rock 'n Roll World Tour	It's a Dog's Life

Figure A7 Sample Middle School Master Schedule – Submitted by E. Lawson Brown Middle School, Davidson County.

Appendix

ELA Remediation Weekly Outline

Day 1: Standard(s). Description/Goal of Standard(s)

Whole Group:

Independent Practice:

Closing:

Day 2: Standard(s). Description/Goal of Standard(s)

Whole Group:

Independent Practice:

Closing:

Day 3:....

 Figure A8   Targeted Instruction Lesson Outline.

During the school-wide intervention block, the school leadership team chose to implement an alternating schedule for reading and math interventions. For example during a four week reading period, all teachers are involved in supporting students in their Reading skills. A reading specialist or a teacher who is certified in middle grades English Language Arts serves our lowest performing students with targeted interventions that were based on a diagnostic software. Teachers who are certified in other content areas focus on comprehension skills with lessons being provided by the reading specialist. Members of our physical education, CTE, and ENCORE (art, music, band) teams involved high performing students in project based learning where 21st Century Skills are incorporated. The projects were engaging and of high interest. Some of the learning opportunities that students selected from were That's Debatable, where students debated current events, Race to the Sun involving research of the solar system, and Bad Boys of History, which focused on the history of famous pirates.

When organizing an intervention block of this nature, many hours and obstacles should be anticipated. It is not an easy task, by any means, but can be done and is well worth it in the long run.

Christa DiBonaventura – Principal, E Lawson Brown Middle School

Appendix

9th Grade Spartan Academy

Teacher	Fall 2016				Spring 2017			
	1st Period	2nd Period	3rd Period	4th Period	1st Period	2nd Period	3rd Period	4th Period
English A	English 1	Yearbook		English 1		Yearbook	English 1	English 1 Honors
English B	English 1	English 1 Honors		English 1 Honors		English 1	English 1	English 1
Math A	Math 1	Foundations Math 1	Foundations Math 1		Math 1 (180)	Math 1 (180)		Math 1 (180)
Math B	Math 2 Honors (9)	Foundations Math 1	Foundations Math 1		Math 1 (180)	Math 1 (180)		Math 1 (180)
Math C	Foundations Math 1	Foundations Math 1	Foundations Math 1		Math 2 (9)	Math 1 (180)		Math 1 (90)
Science A		Earth/ Environ. Science	Earth/ Environ. Science Honors	Earth/ Environ. Science	Earth/ Environ. Science	Earth/ Environ. Science	Earth/ Environ. Science	
Science B		Earth/ Environ. Science	Earth/ Environ. Science Honors	Biology Honors (9)	Earth/ Environ. Science	Biology Honors	Earth/ Environ. Science	
Social Studies A	World History		World History Honors	World History	World History Honors		World History	World History Honors
Social Studies B	World History Honors		World History	World History	World History		World History Honors	World History
Exceptional Children Teachers	English 1 & Foundations of Math	Foundations of Math		English 1	Math 1	Math 1	English 1	English 1

The 9th Grade Spartan Academy is a freshman academy designed to promote student success. The schedule at Central Davidson High School is arranged so that teachers can group and regroup students as needed throughout the year. This is made possible by limiting the number of teachers

Figure A9 Sample High School Master Schedule – Submitted by Central Davidson High School, Davidson County.

who teach our freshmen courses. Teachers are expected to work together to assess students and then form intervention groups as needed, whether it be daily, weekly or by unit. This schedule allows for free movement of students between teachers to intervene when proficiency is not met or to maintain and enrich when it is met. During periods when a common course is not taught, the teachers will utilize exceptional children's teachers and online tutorials to form intervention groups.

Biology								
Fall 2015					Spring 2016			
Teacher	1st Period	2nd Period	3rd Period	4th Period	1st Period	2nd Period	3rd Period	4th Period
Biology A	Biology Honors	Biology Honors		Biology	Biology		Biology Honors	Biology
Biology B		Biology Honors	Biology Honors	Biology Honors		Biology	Biology	Anatomy

In this example, the two Biology teachers planned together and created common assessments. Again, by minimizing the number of teachers teaching a single course, teachers are able to group and regroup students as needed. After assessments, students were grouped by proficiency on specific objectives. Three groups were created after each assessment: those students needing remediation met with the teacher who demonstrated higher proficiency on the objective, those students needing enrichment were grouped with the second teacher for an additional lab activity, and students needing to maintain progress were enrolled in online tutorials to reteach and reassess the objectives covered during the unit.

Both of these examples allow the teachers at Central Davidson High Schools to provide targeted instruction to our students in a fluid and ongoing manner while maintaining pacing and curricular.

Source: Valerie Feezor, Principal, Central Davidson High School

Figure A9 (*Continued*).

Appendix

West Iredell High School
Bell Schedule
2015–2016
MONDAY, TUESDAY, THURSDAY, and FRIDAY

1st Block   8:15am–9:40am (85 min.)

2nd period one-minute warning bell—9:44am

2nd Block   9:45am–11:10am (85 min.)

Return to 1st (Monday)
2nd (Tuesday)
3rd (Thursday)
4th (Friday)   11:15am–11:20am

SWAG (Targeted Instruction)   11:20am–12:15pm (55 min.)

A-Part   11:20am–1:45am
B-Part   11:45am–12:15pm

3rd period one-minute warning bell—12:19pm

3rd Block   12:20pm–1:45pm (85 min.)

4th period one-minute warning bell—1:49pm

4th Block   1:50pm–3:15pm (85 min.)

Figure A10   Sample High School Master Schedule (A) – Submitted by West Iredell High School, Iredell County.

Appendix

```
┌─────────────────────────────────────────────────────────────────────┐
│                      West Iredell High School                         │
│                           Bell Schedule                               │
│                            2015–2016                                  │
│                         WEDNESDAY ONLY                                │
│                                                                       │
│ 1st Block                              8:15am–9:35am (80 min.)         │
│                                                                       │
│             2nd period one-minute warning bell—9:39am                 │
│                                                                       │
│ 2nd Block                              9:40am–11:00am (80 min.)        │
│                                                                       │
│             AA period one-minute warning bell—11:04am                 │
│                                                                       │
│ Advisor/Advisee                        11:05am–11:30am (20 min.)       │
│                                                                       │
│ SWAG                                   11:30am–12:25pm (55 min.)       │
│                                                                       │
│           A-Part          11:30am – 11:55am                           │
│           B-Part          11:55am – 12:25pm                           │
│                                                                       │
│             3rd period one-minute warning bell—12:29pm                │
│                                                                       │
│ 3rd Block                              12:30pm–1:50pm (80 min.)        │
│                                                                       │
│             4th period one-minute warning bell—1:54pm                 │
│ 4th Block                              1:55pm–3:15pm (80 min.)         │
└─────────────────────────────────────────────────────────────────────┘
```

Figure A11   Sample High School Master Schedule (B) – Submitted by West Iredell High School, Iredell County.

Appendix

Our remediation time is focused on mastery in content specific areas. Our targeted instruction block (SWAG) is designed to provide additional support to our students in each of our content areas. This schedule allows all of our content specific experts an opportunity to meet the needs of their students. All students that have less than an 80% class average are required to receive remediation during this time. On a four block schedule we take one day per class (Monday = 1st block, Tuesday = 2nd block, Thursday = 3rd block, Friday = 4th block) with one open day for students to meet with their academic adviser (homeroom teacher) on Wednesdays where students review their grades and attendance.

The schedule is utilized using our SMART Lunch that consists of an hour between 2nd and 3rd block. Smart lunch A is 30 minutes of remediation and SMART Lunch B is 30 minutes for lunch. There are ways of adjusting this for clubs, activities, and intramural sports as well, this ensures that every student has some place to be while also ensuring that they have an opportunity to participate in the clubs and activities they are interested in without having to worry about transportation.

This schedule allows the student's teacher a minimum of 30 additional minutes of tutor time every week. The teacher can also use additional days such as Wednesday homeroom days, and days the student has free from passing other classes. The teacher has multiple data points available for them to understand what gaps need to be focused on, this is something a tutor unfamiliar with the student would lack.

Taking the time to properly plan and monitor our SMART Lunch has allowed us to establish strong organizational structures that have helped to facilitate continual student growth and engagement. It has taken both time and thoughtful planning to properly integrate this time into our schedule, but the benefits have been well worth the effort.

Gordon Palmer – Principal, West Iredell High School